Give the Ballot to the Mothers:
Songs of the Suffragists

A History in Song

WOMEN FINDING THEIR VOICE

These songs are meant to be sung. Pass the lyrics around--one for each person and as you do, think of the women of the 1850's and 1860's who were prohibited from speaking in public, yet sang suffrage songs in their private parlors. Sing these songs in your organizational programs and as you do, think of the women in the 1870's who were inspired by including songs as part of the official agenda of their suffrage association meetings. Perform these songs in choruses and in front of groups, and as you sing out, think of the singing Hutchinsons who traveled the country in the late nineteenth century, who by adding their own suffrage songs to their popular repertoire, helped to convince others of the cause. And finally, have fun singing the vaudevillian style songs of the early twentieth century knowing you are expressing the voices of a widespread popular mass movement--voices which have been overlooked by history and entirely forgotten by musicians.

Francie Wolff

Give the Ballot to the Mothers: Songs of the Suffragists

A History in Song

BY

FRANCIE WOLFF

With a Foreword by
Sheila Tobias

Denlinger's Publishers, Ltd.   Ozark Division   Springfield, Missouri

Denlinger's Publishers, Ltd.
Ozark Division
P.O. Box 4769
Springfield, Missouri 65808

ISBN 0-87714-191-6

This book was completely manufactured in the United States of America.

A *wraparound spiral binding* was chosen for this publication with the intent to create a book that is both aesthetically pleasing in form and practical in application. The color-coordinated spine-covered spiral is designed to make the book appear attractive when placed on a shelf or coffee table, yet with this binding the book will lay flat if it is positioned on a piano or music stand with the pages opened.

printed by Western Printing Company, Inc. Republic, Mo 65738

DEDICATION

To all of the mothers of suffragists.

And to the memory of my own mother,

Lena Rosen

who dedicated her life
to being a wife and mother
and did a good job of it.

TABLE OF CONTENTS

RALLY SONGS

SONGS OF PERSUASION:

POPULAR SONGS:

UPDATE: THE YELLOW RIBBON

ACKNOWLEDGMENTS

John Ruskin said, **"When skill and love work together expect a masterpiece."** I have these words pasted above my desk to serve as a reminder of the qualities which make a work a success. All of the contributors acknowledged below possess the competence and dedication required to fulfill Ruskin's expectations of a masterpiece. However, it is the spirit of the **suffragists**, with their commitment to gain the right to vote for women against all odds, which has served as the inspirational force behind this publication. Each person who has donated his or her talent and intellect toward the making of this book has done so with the implicit acknowledgment of the spirit of the suffragist songwriters represented here.

Dr. Peter Collins, Assistant Professor of Music at Southwest Missouri State University (SMSU), has edited the music of the suffragists. My first impression of Peter was of him sitting in front of his piano after I had irreverently spread my "loosely organized" materials all around his office. His head moved back and forth from the original sheet music to the computerized printout of the song while his hands played the melody. "Here is a spot where a note was left out," or, "This is a misprint." he would say. I was in awe and still am. Thank you Peter for your time and scholarly input.

Bjorn Mercer, graduate of the school of Music of SMSU and graduate student at the University of Arizona, entered each song into the computer. Using the "Finale" program he was able to take my xeroxed pages of hodgepodge songs which I had been collecting and stapling together and writing notes on and misplacing and reorganizing and sometimes agonizing over, and produce clean uniform copies of each song. Thank you Bjorn for making order out of mayhem.

Before the songs were standardized by Bjorn, I took them to Boston with me in raw form to my best friend, **Gwindale Cassity**, musician extraordinaire. We sat in front of her Steinway grand with wine glasses in hand, and giggled over the music while she played with gusto and I sang in a mock opera soprano voice. We had fun with the songs, but I came away with some serious notes. For once I will not have to "save" or "download" or "hide" my written words as I so often have done with our intimate e-mail "chats." One more time, for one more major event in my life, Gwindale "I couldn't have done it without you."

I never would have even started this book *or* finished it were it not for **Thelma Spencer**, writer, publisher, mentor. If inspiration could be packaged and sold, Thelma would be a multi- millionaire! I remember sitting with her at *Tiffany's* having the first of what would prove to be many, tea-time discourses. I told her that I had this project that I would like to do, but I couldn't get a publisher, didn't have the time - - whine, whine, whine -- And she undauntingly said, "You know Francie, you can do this yourself." The lightbulb went off in my head then, but she had to pull the switch first. I took it from there, but not without calling her, meeting with her, asking her opinions, seeking her advice, and most of all operating on her continuing and consistent "you can do" fuel. She had an answer for my every question, a resolution for each doubt. Whenever I thought I had come up with some brilliant notion of my own that was complete, she would take it even one step further. She has expanded my imagination, my dreams and my capabilities. Thank you Thelma for your vision.

But even before Thelma motivated me to write this songbook, I had been working with **Dr. William J. Burling**, Doctor of Philosophy and professor of English at SMSU. Bill and I go back quite a long way, to the first time I shyly walked into his recording studio with a gift certificate for one hour of recording time. He didn't laugh at my music. He expertly got it down on tape, but more importantly, he launched me on the path of creative expression which has been pouring out of me ever since I sat in front of the microphone that day in his home. Since then, we have worked together to produce two videos, *The Spirit of Pioneer Women* and *Give the Ballot to the Mothers: Songs of the Suffragists*. He will see these words before they go to press. He will probably tell me that I need to add a period or cut a phrase or re-word a concept in these acknowledgments. Bill's patience, combined with his mastery of the English language and his multi-talents, makes him the ultimate "renaissance man," -- scholar, teacher, musician, and author -- and the only person who could have edited this book for me.

I could never have written this book without the resources of the **Duane G. Meyer Library** of SMSU. As a library employee I literally "have the world at my fingertips" and the library staff to assist me. In my capacity as Interlibrary Loan Supervisor I am sometimes acknowledged in other people's work. Professors, graduate students, and other scholars seem to be very grateful that I can assist them in finding the material which they need for their research. Now it is my turn to thank all of my cohorts in interlibrary loan, particularly **Shannon Conlin**. Shannon had to "bear with me" while I griped and moaned about meeting deadlines; while I piled books and microfilm under my desk and all over my office; while I frantically searched for some illustration or "important" paper which I had misplaced; while I processed material, searched for sources, spoke with people, and fretted about getting this book published. Her steady and reasoned councel helped to get me through it all.

My colleagues in the reference department have been supportive of my efforts as well. **Willa Garrett's** friendship and kind words provided me with the backing and encouragement that I needed to conduct my own research. **Ed DeLong's** support and talents have aided me also. Thanks to Ed, the photo he snapped of me graces the back of this book as well as the coffee mug I carry around. His talents have made my "mug" recognizable when I accidentally leave it in places I shouldn't be drinking coffee, and *now* in places I actually *want* to be known.

I couldn't have put this book together without the talents and support of those people who work in other departments of the library. I want to express my gratitude for the time and effort of **Jeanne Stephens**, graphic designer in Educational Media. Many times I ran downstairs with photos, illustrations, or other graphics in hand, interrupted her work, and asked her if she could fill out a drawing, add some space, make a "box," align an illustration on the page, scan a photo, rework a drawing, etc. -- and worse yet, "have it for me by Monday?" All the graphic layouts and designs of this book are a result of her skilled artistic endeavors.

And just across the hall, I would dash over to the microforms department with a color illustration or a murky black and white photo and ask **Rita Garrison** if she could "copy, enchance, enlarge, reduce, or "otherwise improve upon" my material. Were it not for her "enhancement" capabilities the book would not have the photos and illustrations it has. Rita not only knows the right buttons to push but also knows the right words of advice and encouragement to give for good results.

Of course none of these talented library employees would feel comfortable encouraging me or giving me special consideration were it not for the support of **Karen Horny**, Dean of Library Services of SMSU. She has set a positive tone for everyone working in the library by recognizing each of our accomplishments.

Finally, I owe a debt of gratitude to my sensitive and insightful son, **Leroy Rottmann**, who has had to live with my obsessive, quirky behavior all these years. Because he is a creative person himself and often launches on his own artistic endeavors, he understands how I can become consumed with a project. But, more than that, his advice at crucial moments has been invaluable; particularly his imaginative input regarding the design of the cover and layout of the pages.

A special aknowledgment to **Dr. Danny O. Crewe**
whose private collection was the source of many of the songs in this book.

FOREWORD

Imagine, if you can, wave upon wave of properly dressed women, young and old, gloved and hatted as was expected of them when they were out of their homes, arms linked, their prim and powdered faces raised in song. They march perhaps in front of a state capitol, or down New York's Fifth Avenue, or perhaps it's just a rally for Women's Suffrage in a rented space or a public park.

You can read determination in their stride, unity in their faces. They are marching for a cause they called "women's rights." Not yet driven to chain themselves to government property or to commit civil disobedience for their cause (that will come later as patience wears thin), they hope to win supporters among the gawkers, and by persistence and persuasion to make victory eventually theirs. They sing:

> "...Who holds that Woman hath no part
> Nor place in council grave
> Who holds that Man alone is 'smart'
> And pure and wise and brave
> ...The day is come when women vote
> ...Just our simple right"

A "Century of Struggle" historian Eleanor Flexner called it[1] and, indeed, bizarre as it seems to the generations who came of age after 1920, the battle for women's right to vote took seventy-five years, from the first stirrings of a few undaunted women in the 1840s and 1850s until the National American Women's Suffrage Association, two-million members strong, carried the day in 1920. The truth is that women's suffrage was no gift from America's male establishment -- to the very end President Woodrow Wilson, a promoter of "self-determination" everywhere in the world but at home among American women, resisted -- but a decades-long series of battles, at the state and national levels, against powerful interests determined to keep women in their "place," even against some women who thought they would be better off without the power that comes with voting. (They were called in the parlance of the times, the "Anti's".)

We know a lot more now about the history of America's suffrage movement than we used to. America's "second-wave" feminists, who came of age after 1967, dubbed the suffrage movement the "first wave," and returned again and again to its roots and to its evolution as researchers and writers. Not that there were no histories before. Contemporary historians, including some of its own leaders, chronicled everything from the foremothers' stirring manifestoes to the day-to-day details of organization. But much of that history -- because of changing attitudes, the Great Depression, and World War II -- was eclipsed during the long dormant period from 1920 to 1967.

---

[1] Eleanor Flexner, <u>Century of Struggle, The Women's Rights Movement in the United States,</u> (Cambridge: Belknap Press, 1975).

What we haven't had until now, with this extraordinary collection of Suffrage Songs, not in the older histories and biographies, not in the new, have been their voices. Absent recording devices (the phonograph, film, and video came later), we have no record of the <u>sound</u> of these suffrage activists, neither their speech individually as they rallied their followers at countless public meetings and events, nor their voices collectively as they cheered and chanted and sang.

Here at last in remarkable purity are twenty-six songs, complete with words and music (some of the lyrics joined to familiar melodies that we will recognize even today) just as the suffragists would have rendered them in the last decades of their struggle. Thanks to the indefatigable searches of musician and librarian Francie Wolff, we can read the lyrics, play the melodies, and <u>hear</u> what they must have sounded like, sung in chorus. All this will make it easier for us henceforth to conjure up the settings in which these suffrage songs first were sung.

Wolff has provided comments and annotations both about the musical history of the songs in this collection and about how they were used. There were, she tells us, songs specifically sung at rallies: songs meant to persuade; songs about the "suffragette" herself (even a few hostile barbs.) But most of the songs, like those who sung them, were positive and optimistic. For, by the time the songs in this collection were being sung, support for women's voting rights was, at least among women and far-sighted men, widespread. Women's suffrage had been endorsed by the General Federation of Women's Clubs and two million women were on record as supporting what would become the 19th amendment to the Constitution.

==========

To be sure, the Nineteenth Amendment no more guaranteed suffrage for <u>all</u> women any more than the Constitution -- amended after slavery was abolished to include Negro <u>males</u> -- guaranteed voting rights for all men. America in 1920 was a society divided in its privileges by race, class, and immigrant status. Barriers to voting, such as the poll tax and education and property qualifications, effectively blocked racial minorities from the polls, especially in the South. It is for this reason that most radical historians (along with second-wave feminists and women of color) regard the passage of the 1974 amendments to the 1965 Voter Registration Act, which guaranteed access to the polls for all citizens in all sections of the country, of far greater import than the women's suffrage amendment passed fifty-four years before.

Still, women's suffrage was significant, as a first step toward equality and shared responsibility for the country in which we all reside; and as a symbol. The suffrage leaders knew this and while they promised more than they could possibly deliver -- politics without corruption, a world without war -- they set the stage for the participation of women in politics which has led, in our own time, to the appointments of Sandra Day O'Connor and Ruth Bader Ginsburg to the Supreme Court, of Janet Reno to the position of U.S. Attorney General, to Madeline Albright as Secretary of State, and to the election and appointment of hundreds of women to legislatures and policy-making positions in state and local government.

Why did the Suffragists sing? one is tempted to ask. Why not simply rant and rave and hack away at male privilege? One reason is tradition: American women's rightists were bred on song. There was a hymnal in every Protestant church pew and some kind of musical instrument at home -- a piano for those who could afford it -- around which family and friends would gather for song and celebration. Then, too, song is spirited, and stirs the heart. Soldiers march to rallying songs. America's slave population sang to show their solidarity and to survive; union members struggling to make their voices heard did the same.

In recent memory, songs like "We Shall Overcome" and "If I had a Hammer" presented another century's reformers with the means to state a shared commitment in another century's struggles for civil rights and against the War in Vietnam. Singers like Woody Guthrie, Pete Seeger, and the group Peter, Paul, and Mary will be remembered, I am sure, not just for their wonderful singing but for having brought politics back into song.[2]

Even second-wave feminists have had their singers and their songs. In Here's to the Women: 100 Songs for and about American Women, collectors Hilda E. Wenner and Elizabeth Freilicher,[3] remind us that women's liberation, knowingly or not, built on the choral tradition of the Suffragists. Surely Helen Reddy's "I am Woman, Hear me Roar" will go down in history as a "rally" song for my generation of feminists as played (if not sung) at second-wave feminist rallies, as will Holly Near's and Peggy Seeger's music and lyrics.

Francie Wolff is not just a collector. She is a musician and lyricist in her own right and the songs she has written and performs (songs not included in this collection) are intended to inspire young women to create their own "third wave" of feminist activism. With this volume, she reminds us -- as my generation of feminists needs to be reminded -- that Sisterhood for our foremothers was as much a source of passion and power as it has been for us.

Sheila Tobias
Tuscon, Arizona - July, 1997

Sheila Tobias is author of *Faces of Feminism: An Activist's Reflections on the Women's Movement* (Westview Press, 1997)

---

[2] Even today, certain chapters of the American Association of University Women end their meetings with song.

[3] The Feminist Press, 1987

Suffrage News

SATURDAY, DECEMBER 11, 1915   **FIVE CENTS**

WILL CONGRESS HEED?

Fredrikke S. Palmer.

INTRODUCTION

"A history of America, vivid, dramatic, and personal, could be written with the songs of its people." This statement introduces "American Folksongs of Protest," John Greenway's definitive book on the subject, yet not one suffrage song is mentioned in the book. The songs of the American Woman Suffrage Movement were also "vivid, dramatic, and personal" but have been forgotten and overlooked by chroniclers of American protest music just as the suffrage movement itself has been forgotten and overlooked by historians. A bare smattering of suffrage songs can be found in a few American music anthologies, but generally speaking, these songs have not been noted in the annals of popular American music, even though in their time, some of them were widely known.

This book is the first to publish these songs and their music together under one cover. During the suffrage movement itself some suffrage songs were published as ephemera, but because they were mostly sung to familiar tunes, they contained no musical notations. An album, "Songs of the Suffragettes" (Folkways Records, 1958) features many of the early suffrage songs but again published only the lyrics alongside historical commentary. And in 1974 a collection of photocopied songs entitled, "Songs of Suffrage" (Deliverance Press, Kalamazoo, Michigan) also presented the lyrics only, and included none of the later songs.

The history of these suffrage songs is entwined with the history of popular American music. As the suffrage movement gained momentum and became a popular mass movement in the early twentieth century, the music publishing business itself boomed, as songsters marketed sheet music to the masses from Tin Pan Alley while at the same time minstrel shows and vaudeville musicals were creating popular music literally by the scores. Suffrage songs, which by that time also represented mass sentiment, took on the form of the popular music of the day, so that one can find such odd combinations as a minstrel-style suffrage song, a ragtime suffrage song, and even a suffrage song written specifically for the Zeigfeld Follies. The stilted rally songs which reflected the Victorian musical style known by the first suffragists, who were then going against the tide of popular sentiment, gave way to the jazzier popular tunes sung by the masses in the twentieth century. This wide variety of musical style of songs about female suffrage owes itself to the 75-year-long protracted struggle of the suffrage movement.

The quality of the suffrage songs varies since they were, for the most part written and sung by amateurs. Many of them are musically and harmonically stilted and some of the lyrics are dated and contrived, but they are nonetheless important documents of protest and rhetorical thought. They represent the voices of thousands of people who were part of a significant movement in United States history.

RALLY SONGS

Votes for Women

Suffrage Rallying Song

LIBERTY

Words By
EDW. M. ZIMMERMAN
Music By
MARIE ZIMMERMAN

Price 10¢

Published by

E. M. ZIMMERMAN
1710 CHESTNUT ST.
PHILADELPHIA, PA.

THE GREAT EQUAL SUFFRAGE CAMPAIGN SONG

V O T E S

W O M E N

Dedicated to the Universal Cause of Equal Suffrage

JUSTICE: Woman, go take with Man thy rightful place.
Do thy full duty well, and help protect the race.

FOR

WORDS AND MUSIC BY

MARY LOUISE CARLETON

PUBLISHED BY

THE CALIFORNIA MUSIC PRESS

SAN LEANDRO, CALIFORNIA

Price 25c Net; 3 Copies 60c; 10 Copies $1.75.   Mailed Postpaid in U. S. A.

RALLY SONGS

Rally songs were meant to inspire or to rouse women to action and were usually sung to the tunes of familiar songs. That way, when the lyrics were passed around, people could easily join in on the singing because they already knew the melody. The familiar hymn and the patriotic anthem were the two most common types employed by suffragists.

The melody was often that of a *familiar hymn* because hymns were the form of music which were commonly known and readily available, particularly to the early Suffragists. In fact the first American popular songs were the psalms and hymns which flourished in New England among the colonists. After the American Revolution, sacred music became even more popularized when Lowell Mason published *The Boston Handel and Haydn Society of Church Music*. Mason also introduced music into the Boston schools and composed more than 1200 hymns himself.

Hymns were more than merely convenient, as many early suffrage leaders were religious leaders as well. Lucretia Mott, one of the organizers of the first Women's Rights Convention held in Seneca Falls in 1848 was a devout Quaker, and Reverend Olympia Brown, who was the oldest living suffragist when the 19th Amendment was finally passed in 1920, was a minister of the Universalist Church and the first denominationally ordained female minister in the United States.

THE OLDEST AND THE YOUNGEST
Rev. Olympia Brown and Miss Rowena Green at the Republican Convention, Chicago, 1920
(National Woman's Party)

Although it was natural for suffragists to turn to religion for inspiration, anti-suffragists and church leaders also often pointed to the Bible to make a case *against* suffrage for women. In fact, Elizabeth Cady Stanton, who was one of the original organizers of the first Women's Rights Convention held in Seneca Falls in 1848, and the first president of the National American Woman Suffrage Association (NAWSA) in 1890, condemned the clergy and publicly denounced the Bible. She wrote her own version of the Bible called, *The Woman's Bible* and its publication caused great controversy and division among those supporting suffrage for women.

Early suffragists often fashioned their gatherings after prayer meetings because church functions were among the few accessible and acceptable opportunities for women to gather at that time. And, like church meetings, *song* was an integral part of the agenda of these suffragist gatherings. *A Manual for Political Equality Clubs* published in 1896 by the American Woman Suffrage Association features a "responsive reading" by the president, vice-president, secretary, and treasurer, and urges that "all present should join in the singing." Eleven different suffrage songs are featured in part or whole in this early manual for suffragists.

This official use of song in meetings lasted throughout the entire 75-year-long struggle. The minutes of the last meeting of the National American Woman Suffrage Association (NAWSA) held in St. Louis in 1919 attest to this practice:

> The Chair called the convention to order at 8 o'clock
> Invocation by Dr. Shaw
> Community *singing* led by Mrs. W .D. Steele.

Dr. Anna Howard Shaw, referred to above, was another lifelong suffragist leader and was also the first woman to become an ordained minister of the Methodist Church. She died four months after giving the invocation for that famous final meeting in 1919 in which Carrie Chapman Catt, the president of NAWSA, disbanded the organization and called for the formation of a new group, "The League of Women Voters."

Even the more militant group, the National Woman's Party, which existed alongside the NAWSA from 1913-1919, turned to hymns to propound their rhetoric. The Party's official motto was *Forward out of Darkness, Forward Into Light,* which was a phrase taken directly from the cantata "Forward into Light," an aria from *The Celestial Country* written by Charles Ives in 1889. The slogan was emblazoned on banners and signs and seen in picket-lines and parades.

Inez Milholland Leading first
Suffrage Procession at National
Capital, March, 1913.
(National Woman's Party)

Inez Milholland, who was a labor lawyer, a social reformer, and a passionate activist for suffrage, led suffrage parades while carrying the golden banner with the inspirational words urging women to march *"forward into light."* She presented a beautiful image as a herald dressed in white flowing robes riding atop a white horse. Inez rigorously campaigned for suffrage in spite of her poor health and was finally hailed a martyr for the cause when she collapsed on the podium in Los Angeles during a strenuous cross-country speaking tour. With 10,000 people attending, she was the first woman to be given a memorial service in the nation's Capitol.

One melody which was used over and over with many different sets of suffrage lyrics was the "Battle Hymn of the Republic." Three different sets of suffrage lyrics were published to this melody alone in the 1884 *Booklet of song: A Collection of Suffrage and Temperance Melodies.* This familiar melody was originally a camp meeting hymn written by William Steffe around 1856 and was known as "Glory Hallelujah." The first line to the song was, "Say, brothers will you meet us?" During the Civil War the tune was popularly sung by Union soldiers as, "John Brown's Body." Then Julia Ward Howe elevated the song in 1862 by writing the famous lyrics, "Battle Hymn of the Republic." The story of how Mrs. Howe came to write the lyrics is recounted by Sigmund Spaeth in, *A History of Popular Music in America*:

> Mrs. Howe and her husband were in Washington when they heard some soldiers singing *John Brown's Body* to the familiar *Glory Hallelujah* tune. The Rev. James Freeman Clarke, who was with them, asked Mrs. Howe if she could not think up some more worthy text for the rousing melody. That night at the Willard Hotel the opening line of the poem, "Mine eyes have seen the glory of the coming of the Lord," came to her in her sleep. She lighted [sic] a candle, and before dawn the entire text was completed, an inspiration as direct as any in history.
>
> Mrs. Howe sold her poem to the *Atlantic Monthly* for ten dollars, and it appeared on the front page of the February issue of 1862. It was promptly reprinted in a number of newspapers and soon appeared in the army hymn-books (Spaeth, p.148)

It should be noted that Julia Ward Howe was also a dedicated suffragist and was first president of the New England Woman Suffrage Association established in 1868. She was very active in the American Woman Suffrage Association, which was an organization existing alongside the National Woman Suffrage Association for 21 years until the two merged in 1890 to become the National American Woman Suffrage Association. Mrs. Howe, an ardent Unitarian, fervently believed that religion and female suffrage went hand in hand. In one of her speeches she stated,

> The weapon of Christian warfare is the ballot, which represents the peaceable assertion of conviction and will. Adopt it. O you women, with clean hands and a pure heart!

It is in this spirit that the rousing "Battle Hymn of the Republic" was adapted for the suffrage movement in this "Hallelujah Song:"

> Our hearts have felt the glory of the coming of the time,
> When law and right and love and might shall make our land sublime,
> When mount and hill and rock and rill with freedom's light will shine,
> As Truth comes marching on.
>
> CHORUS--Glory, glory hallelujah!
> Glory, glory hallelujah!
> Glory, glory hallelujuah!
> As Truth comes marching on.

They saw it in the shadows of that old New England Bay,
They heard it in the breezes of that cold December day,
They sent it with the echoes to Britannia far away,
That Truth was marching on.--CHORUS

The trumpet then was sounded that shall never call retreat;
Adown the cent'ries softly we hear the tramp of feet;
Today we still are marching to the same old music sweet,
Of Truth still marching on.--CHORUS.

We're here to swell the anthem that is heard across the sea,
That equal rights in law and love is meant for you and me,
Where every law was founded on the plane of liberty
While Truth came marching on.--CHORUS.

L. May Wheeler, 1884

A later adaptation, "The Battle Hymn of the Suffragists" written by Frances Weed Campbell in memory of Matilda Joslyn Gage, an early suffragist who worked with Susan B. Anthony, appears in *The Woman's Journal*. This version, while expressed in slightly more modern language, still has women tirelessly marching on to the "same old sweet music."

They come from every nation, women fair and strong and brave.
They come with zeal so holy all the weaker ones to save.
To turn the helpless children back from darkness and the grave.
Their cause is marching on.

CHORUS--Glory, Glory Hallelujah.
       Glory, Glory Hallelujah.
       Glory, Glory Hallelujah.
       Their cause is marching on.

They will not be disheartened by the taunts and jibes and jeers
Of those who would oppose them, for they've lost the foolish fears
That once belonged to women, the women of past years,
And their hearts are brave and strong. -- CHORUS

They hope to make the women stand for all that's just and right,
And so they wage their warfare keen with all their woman's might.
Hoping soon injustice will give place to freedom bright,
And their great cause be won -- CHORUS.

Besides religious music, patriotic songs were the other early form of popular American music. Thus many suffrage rally songs were sung to the tunes of **patriotic anthems** such as "America," "The National Anthem" or "The Red White and Blue." These familiar melodies reenforced the argument that woman suffrage was a patriotic cause. Typically, such songs would take the concepts in the titles and lyrics from these revered anthems and apply them to the cause of suffrage. In this way "The Star Spangled Banner" became "The Equal Rights Banner," which was one of the songs printed in the 1896 *Manual for Political Equality Clubs*:

Oh say, have you heard of the new, dawning light,
Bringing hope to our land, and its foes all surprising?
Our banner still floats, as the emblem of right,
And the day breaks upon us, for women are rising.

CHORUS-And with ballots in hand, at the right's dear command,
They'll be true to the flag and will rescue our land;
And ever the Equal Rights Banner shall wave
O'er the land of the free and the home of the brave.

Woman's ballot is just, so then conquer we must,
And this be our watchword, "In God is our trust."
And our Equal Rights Banner in triumph shall wave
O'er the land of the free and the home of the brave.--CHORUS

Rev. C.C. Harrah.

And "America" became "The New America," which was one of the songs printed in the program of the NAWSA convention of 1891:

Our country, now from thee
Claim we our liberty,
In freedom's name.
Guarding home's altar fires,
Daughters of patriot sires,
Their zeal our own inspires
Justice to claim.

Women in every age
For this great heritage
Tribute have paid
Our birth-right claim we now --
Longer refuse to bow;
On freedom's altar now
Our hand is laid.

Sons, will you longer see,
Mothers on bended knee
For justice pray?
Rise now, in manhood's might,
With earth's great souls unite
To speed the dawning light
Of freedom's day.

Elizabeth Boynton Herbert.

However, not all rally songs were sung to familiar tunes. Some had *original melodies*. Since most of these rally songs were written by amateur musicians, the music was sometimes primitive, contrived and lacking in sophistication. Some songs contained misprints because they were notated by hand and not thoroughly edited. The most glaring of these errors are corrected or annotated here.

Original suffrage rally songs are typically two-part marches consisting of the *verse* leading to the rousing *chorus*. The verses of these songs are not intended to be particularly musical, but serve as a vehicle to set the stage or present the theme of the chorus. Melody components usually include a brief instrumental introduction, interludes of interpretive "bugle calls" and "drum rolls" throughout the song, and a dramatic, soaring ending.

The lyrics of original rally songs often used rhetoric borrowed from church music, using words like, "lo, hark, won'drous, 'mongst, 'twas, and glorious." Military or patriotic rhetoric was also employed with the use of such terms as, "victory, battle, triumph, and sovereign."

Legions of women literally marched to the tunes of these rousing *Suffrage Rally Songs* in grandly-staged parades and picket lines, and were stirred to action by the inspirational lyrics in their meetings and rallies.

20,000 women marched in New York City's suffrage parade, 1915 (Library of Congress)

GIVE THE BALLOT TO THE MOTHERS - Rebecca N. Hazard to the tune of "Marching Through Georgia"

The psychologists tell us that no word in the English language has more emotional appeal or positive association than "mother." And even though the woman's suffrage movement pre-dates Freudian psychology, the proponents of votes for women must have had an insight into this fundamental psychological truth. The song literature of the suffrage movement abounds with references to "mothers" voting -- and even those who were unmoved by pleas for women's rights at the ballot box could not help but feel some twinge of conscience at the thought of denying a fundamental right to "mother" (program notes, "Songs of the Suffragettes," Folkway Records, 1958).

However, the anti-suffragists also made an appeal to motherhood. They claimed that once women got the vote, the family and society itself would crumble.

Both groups had *Mom* on their side.

(Library of Congress)

The melody, "Marching through Georgia" was originally a Civil War song published in 1856. The "gaiety of the music". . . has made it a "college favorite, with Princeton turning it to the most practical use as a football song" (Spaeth, *A History of Popular Music in America,*157).

This combination of direct lyrics and catchy melody makes "Give the Ballot to the Mothers" a classic and very "singable" suffrage rally song.

12

Give the Ballot to the Mothers

Words: Rebecca N. Hazard

Music: Marching through Georgia
by Henry Work

GIVE MOTHER THE VOTE

WE NEED IT

OUR FOOD   OUR HEALTH   OUR PLAY
OUR HOMES   OUR SCHOOLS   OUR WORK
ARE   RULED   BY   MEN'S   VOTES

Isn't it a funny thing
That Father cannot see
Why Mother ought to have a vote
On how these things should be?

THINK IT OVER

Rose O'Neill, creator of the popular kewpie dolls, was a suffragist. She designed postcards and posters for the National American Woman Suffrage Publishing Company from 1910 to 1920. The above illustration is a facsimile of one such poster. The marching babies depicted are Kewpie-like fully dressed toddlers with cherubic faces. O'Neill used her already popular images to make a visual statement about suffrage which would appeal to her fans.

THE SUFFRAGE FLAG - William P. Adkinson to the tune of "Bonnie Blue Flag"

Flags and banners have served to solidify political movements throughout the ages, and the American Woman Suffrage Movement was no exception to this rule. The illustration of the flag as shown below appeared in the National American Woman Suffrage Association *Headquarter News,* September 22, 1916 with the following description:

. . . The banner has a gold background with an eagle in the center, surrounded by eleven blue stars, representing the eleven full suffrage states. This national flag may be adopted as a state flag by each organization, the eagle in that case to be substituted by the state emblem . . . We feel that the suffrage movement should have one flag for all and all should be for one flag, and we trust that this flag . . . may soon wave over a 'Solid America' -- solid for suffrage . . . because we realize that the political boss glories in division of opposition, and it is only by union that we go on to speedy victory. We want this movement to have one body, one name, one purpose, for then our victory will come speedily, and then we will teach the people of this country that suffrage is the paramount issue of the day.

The National Woman's Party (NWP) also had a suffrage banner with each star representing a state which had voted for suffrage. Flags and banners with the NWP colors of purple, white, and gold were carried in parades, rallies and picket lines.

The melody "Bonnie Blue Flag" was a Civil War song and was the semiofficial national anthem of the Confederacy. It was published under an act of congress of the Confederate States in the District of Louisiana in 1861. The song, written by Harry B. McCarthy was actually fitted to the traditional Irish tune, "The Irish Jaunting Car."

The lyrics of the second verse of "The Suffrage Flag" depict the car (because it rhymes with "star" no doubt) of progress with the suffrage flag waving over the headlights. The "progress" the song refers to is toward that of a world where women will vote and "war shall be at an end."

The Suffrage Flag

Words: William P. Adkinson

Music: Bonnie Blue Flag

bears the wo-man's star._____ Hur - rah!_____ Hur - rah!_____ For e - qual rights Hur -
bears the wo-men's star_____

rah!_____ Hur - rah! For the suf-frage— flag that bears the wo-man's star!_____

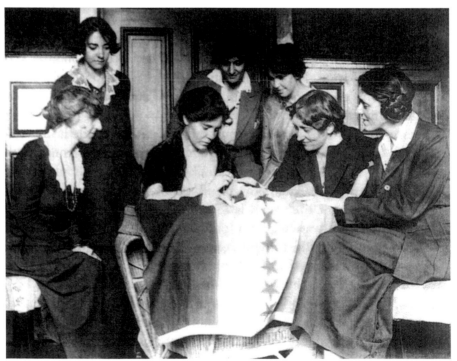

Sewing the final ratification star on the National Woman's Party suffrage banner.
The women include (l to r) Mable Vernon, Elizabeth Kalb, Alice Paul, Florence
Brewer Boeckel, Anita Pollitzer, Sue White, and Vivian Pearce, 1920.
(Schlesinger Library, Radcliff College)

Upon the word that Tennessee had ratified, Alice Paul unfurled the Woman's Party ratification banner with its thirty-six victory stars.

COLUMBIA'S DAUGHTERS - Harriet H. Robinson to the tune of "Hold the Fort"

The program notes accompanying this song in the Folkways Records album, "Songs of the Suffragettes" have this to say about *Columbia's Daughters*:

It is hardly surprising to see the melody of "Hold the Fort" turn up in a collection of suffrage songs, because in the latter half of the 19th Century, no gospel hymn was more popular or more widely sung then this one . . . .
The original "Hold the Fort" was written in 1870 by Philip Paul Bliss who was inspired by the recitation of an account of a Civil War incident in which General Sherman was reputed to have sent a message to a beleaguered garrison: "Hold the fort; I am coming. W. T. Sherman."
The well-known evangelist-gospel singer, Ira D. Sankey, introduced the song to both American and British audiences and it became an overnight sensation. Since then it has been parodied countless times for every conceivable cause.

"Columbia's Daughters" must have been a popular suffrage song as it appears in many suffrage song collections.

Columbia's Daughters

Words: Harriet H. Robinson

Music: Hold the Fort

SUFFRAGE SONG (Let Us Sing As We Go) - Eleanor Smith

This song was one of a collection of *Hull House Songs* published in 1915 in Chicago by the Clayton F. Summy Co. and in London by the Weekes & Co. The Hull House was a settlement house founded in 1889 in Chicago by social reformers Jane Addams and Ellen Gates Starr. It was established primarily as a welfare agency for needy families and had the aim of combating juvenile delinquency by providing recreational facilities for children living in slums. Another purpose of Hull House was to assist immigrants in becoming American citizens.

Jane Addams was also an advocate for women's rights and suffrage. She joined the NAWSA in 1906 and became its vice president in 1911. She traveled extensively, lobbying and writing for the woman suffrage cause. Many women, such as Jane Addams who became involved in the settlement house movement and other areas of social reform, became politically active in order to further their cause, but without the vote their hands were tied.

Although music of social protest was not a type widely known in America in 1915, Jane Addams defines and defends this style of song in the introduction to the *Hull House Songs*:

. . . considering it a legitimate function of the settlement to phrase in music the wide spread social compunctions of our day . . . We believe that all of the songs in this collection fulfill the highest mission of music, first in giving expression to the type of emotional experience which quickly tends to get beyond words, and second in affording an escape from the unnecessary disorder of actual life into the wider region of the spirit . . . Because old-fashioned songs . . . chiefly expressed the essentially individualistic emotions of love, hope or melancholy, it is perhaps all the more imperative that socialized emotions should also find musical expression, if the manifold movements of our contemporaries are to have the inspiration and solace they so obviously need.

This song is one of the more sophisticated and artistically cohesive of the original rally types. The lofty lyrics match the rich harmonies making the song a dramatic success. And the usual elements of original rally songs such as, the march tempo and triumphant "drum rolls" and "bugle calls," are an integral part of the melody. Unlike most other original rally songs, which often have a rather dull musical introduction to a rousing chorus, this entire song is both rousing and memorable.

Jane Addams (far right) in a Suffrage parade, Chicago, 1910 (Jane Addams Memorial Collection, The University Library, The University of Illinois)

Suffrage Song

(Let Us Sing As We Go)

Words: James Weber Linn

Music: Eleanor Smith

Let us sing as we go, Votes for Wo-men! Let us sing as we go, Votes for Wo-men

1. Though the way may be hard, Tho' the bat—tle be long; Yet our tri-umph is sure Put your heart— in-to song: In-to cheer-ing and song Votes for Wo-men!
2. There's a voice we have heard, And shall hear—till we die; By its word we are stirred And as one— we re-ply: It is nigh, it is nigh, Votes for wo-men!

For the right shall pre-vail o-ver

wrong!

See! the ban - ner is bright strea - ming o'er us, And the barred road lies o - pen be -
For the fears of the past lie be - hind us, And its fet - ters no long - er can

fore us; Let the trump - et be blown, Let our pur - pose be known, Put your voice and your soul in the
bind us; Let us march with a will Till the trump - et be still In the peace that our strug - gle shall

cho - rus!
find us.

Let us sing as we go, Votes for

Wo - men! Let us sing as we go, Votes for Wo - men! Though the way may be hard, Tho' the

24

batt - tle be long, Yet our tri - umph is sure; put your heart— in - to song, In - to cheer - ing and song: Votes for

wo - men! For the right shall pre - vail o - ver wrong!

MARCHING ON TO VICTORY - Schuyler Green/Otto Motzan

The "Religioso" verse of this song sets the stage for the "Grandioso" chorus in typical rally song fashion. The lyrics of the verse include hymnal-like words such as "Lo, behold, wondrous, and hark" while the chorus contains war-like rhetoric heralding a "legion Mother army Marching on to Victory." The strength and purpose of motherhood are alluded to several times calling upon "Ev'ry Mothers' Son" and proclaiming that, "We gave the Nation its soldiers."

The intricate and highly developed harmonic progressions show creativity and originality, yet the song still falls into the familiar verse/chorus structure. This memorable and driving chorus no doubt stood alone as a rally cry for Suffragists.

RESPECTFULLY INSCRIBED TO THE SUFFRAGISTS OF THE WORLD

MARCHING ON TO VICTORY

WORDS BY
SCHUYLER GREENE
MUSIC BY
OTTO MOTZAN

VOTES FOR WOMEN

50¢

Published by JOS. W. STERN & CO.

Marching On To Victory

Words: Schuyler Greene

Music: Otto Motzan

Lo be-hold a won-d'rous morn-ing day-light has come at last._____ See those ban-ners "Votes for Wo-men,"
We Shall strive and we shall con-quer, hard tho' the fight may be;_____ And tho' hearts grow weak and wea-ry,

hark to the trum-pet's blast._____ And with the dawn-ing, there comes a warn-ing,
we'll "Hike" from sea to sea._____ Fath-ers and moth-ers, sis-ters and broth-ers,

"Woe to the rule of Knaves." We gave the Na - tions its sol - diers,
join hands a - round the world. Our voic - es ne'er shall be si - lent,

REFRAIN *(Grandioso)*

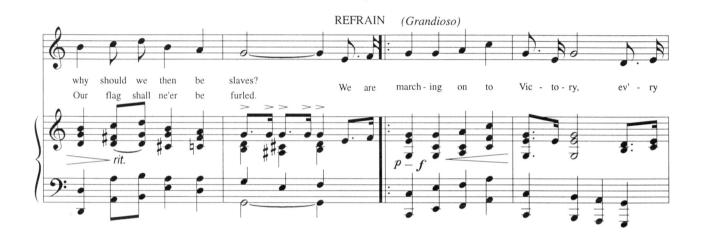

why should we then be slaves? We are march - ing on to Vic - to - ry, ev' - ry
Our flag shall ne'er be furled.

heart is light, For our "Cause" is "Right." We are striv - ing for our lib - er - ty, And we're

here to fight,____ With all our might____ Ev' - ry Moth - ers' Son, Ev' - ry

loy - al one, Sing the praise on land and sea,____ O a leg - ion Moth - er

ar - my, March - ing on to Vic - to - ry.____ We are ory.____

*) F octave in original printing

VOTES FOR WOMEN - Mary Louise Carleton

VOTES FOR WOMEN - Zimmerman and Zimmerman

These two "Votes for Women" were both locally published and were obviously written by amateurs. The lyrics of both songs are contrived and contain a strong moral tone. The awkwardly worded Carleton lyrics purport that granting women the vote will "speed the coming day, when shall become in fact, the plan that God hath had alway." And Zimmerman calls for women to "stoutly pull together to right a grievous wrong!"

Both songs drive home the argument that the injustices of the world will be made right once women have the chance to exert their moral influence by voting. The chorus in the Carelton song proclaims, "But now we see the Light gleaming o'er the land, Justice and Right marching hand in hand . . . the day is come when women vote." Zimmerman even alludes to the specific injustice of child labor: "The joyless haunt of drudges where children toil and die may find these votes the judges that ask the reason why."

Both songs have the familiar two-part verse/chorus structure, framed by an instrumental introduction and coda. In the Carleton song, the verse sets the stage for the chorus with a gentle, lyrical "swing" and the chorus then takes off in a driving eighth and quarter note beat. The Zimmerman song has a drawn-out verse leading up to the chorus which has a traditional hymnal-like conclusion, almost calling for an *Ahhhh...men* at the end.

The music of both these songs is simple and standard using tonic dominant harmonies. An example of an unsophisticated variance of the melody occurs in the Zimmerman song where an attempt is made to sound harmonically darker by changing to a minor key when the lyrics paint a bleaker picture - "enthralling us too long," etc. But both compositions are rather childlike primitive marches.

These two "Votes for Women" attest to the fact that ordinary women and men were aroused by the cause of suffrage. Zimmerman and Zimmerman were probably a husband/wife team and Mary Louise Carleton's song marvelously illustrates the higher purpose of suffrage on the cover by depicting Lady Justice herself giving women the weapon of the ballot with which to slay the wolves of oppression, immorality, and corruption.

These two songs may sound like stilted parodies today, but in their "time" they were most likely both pertinent and inspiring to those women and men who were in the midst of the "battle."

Votes for Women

By: Mary Louise Carleton

There is no realm in earth's do - main, 'Mongst beasts, nor birds, nor
'Twas said not man - y years a - go, By men wise and dis -

bees, Where such un - e - qual code doth reign, As that which Man de -
creet, That wo - men had no souls, you know, But on - ly hands and

crees: Who holds that Wo - man hath no part Nor place in coun - cil
feet. These days we've souls, that's some re - lief, But still the fact re -

grave,   Who holds that Man a - lone is "smart," And pure, and wise, and
mains,   Ac - cord - ing to man's best be - lief, We're sad - ly short of

brave.   Ah! rel - ic of a by - gone age, Shall we thy truth ad -
brains!   Day fol - lows night, and Dark - ness flees, At dawn of Jus - tice

mit?   Shall nev - er Man turn o'er the page On which was er - ror
fair,   When in - e - qual - i - ty shall cease, In coun - cil all may

writ?   Shall we ne'er wak - en from that Night We dwelt in cave and
share.   Why should not wo - man work with Man To speed the com - ing

tree,
When sim - ple force of Might made Right, When Wo - man mute must

day,
When shall be - come in fact, the plan That God hath had al -

CHORUS
Soprano

Alto

But now we see the Light gleam-ing o'er the land, Jus - tice and Right

be?
way?

march-ing hand in hand. Strug - gle on, for vic - to - ry is near, The day is come when wo - men

vote.   Votes for Wo - men!   Just our sim - ple right;   We   want to help to make   the

world more bright.   Men must know   that we   are   tru - ly   work - ing for the good   of

all.

Votes for Women

Suffrage Rallying Song

Words: Edw. M. Zimmerman

Music: Marie Zimmerman

geth - er To right a griev - ous wrong!
judg - es that ask the rea - son why!
e - ver, Press on to vic - to - ry!   Shout the song of "Votes for

Wom - en"! Ring it out up - on the air! Hear its note, ye pa - triot

free - men,_____ Who the right would dare! Sing a loud with lus - ty

vig - or,_____ Till it rat - tles earth and sky, That the wom - an's__ cause grows__

big - ger, And the wom - ans day draws nigh!

(Library of Congress)

SONGS OF PERSUASION

Is It RIGHT?

Song by W. G. FORTNEY

PUBLISHED
BY THE

Macdonald Music Co.
P. O. Box 634 - SAN FRANCISCO

Price 25c net.

WHEN HELEN CASTS HER BALLOT

WORDS BY

JOHN KIRK

MUSIC BY

PETER J. BAST

BAST KIRK MUSIC PUB. CO.
SAN FRANCISCO — OAKLAND
CAL.

Morgan

⑤

SHE'S GOOD ENOUGH TO BE YOUR BABY'S MOTHER

AND SHE'S GOOD ENOUGH TO VOTE WITH YOU

SONG

LYRIC BY
ALFRED BRYAN

MUSIC BY
HERMAN PALEY

5

JEROME H. REMICK & CO.

NEW YORK   DETROIT

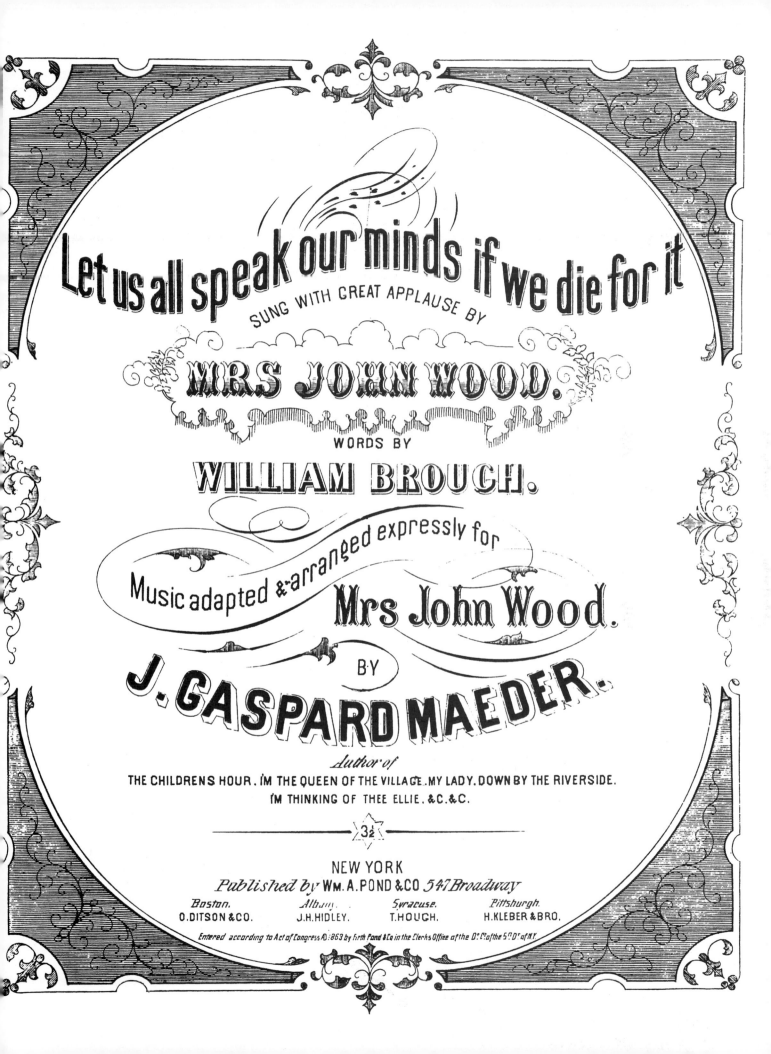

SONGS OF PERSUASION

Songs of persuasion question and argue, urging the listener to "let woman choose her sphere" explaining "why women are wanting the vote." They present the virtues of motherhood and the injustices of taxation without representation, and often propose what the world might be like after women win the vote.

Irwin Silber calls suffrage songs of persuasion *Logical Argument* songs and states that these songs attempted "in one way or another to convince people that woman suffrage is not only a right of the women, but a positive value to the nation and a logical extension of American democracy" (*Sing Out,* Winter 1957, p. 8). However, no Suffragist sat down and said, "Now I think I will write a *logical argument* song." The songs were written spontaneously, in moments of inspiration and reflect, more than any descriptive category, the personal lives of the songwriters and their reaction to the age in which they lived. Thus the attitudes and prejudices of the songwriters and the social milieu of the times are revealed in these persuasive songs.

The song of persuasion is quite similar to the rally song, and at the time these suffrage songs were written no lines of distinction was made between them. S*ongs of persuasion* were also used for rallying purposes, and songs which we now call *rally songs* were sometimes used to persuade. These songs have only recently been categorized and classified by historians and musicologists in order to study them more easily.

A closer look at the song titles themselves shows the difference between a rally song and a song of persuasion. While the rally song title heralds that, *We are Marching on to Victory* and encourages us to . . . *Sing as We Go*, the song of persuasion asks the question, *Is It Right?*, predicts what will happen *When Helen Casts Her Ballot,* and tells us that *If She's Good Enough to Be Your Baby's Mother, She's Good Enough to Vote with You.*

There are common features in the melodies of both types of songs. Both rally songs and songs of persuasion were sometimes written to familiar tunes. And the reasons for using known melodies remain the same for both genres. First, because the melodies are recognizable, the songs are easy to sing. Also, R. Serge Denisoff explains, "the utilization of popular or familiar tunes to which new lyrics are adapted . . . places emphasis on a commonality of experience and speeds communication in terms of a perceived social discontent" (Denisoff, p. 5). While Denisoff neglects to mention suffrage songs in his book, *Sing a Song of Social Significance*, many of his descriptions of protest songs, or *propaganda songs* as he calls them, apply to the protest songs written about suffrage.

Thus the songs of persuasion are perhaps the most interesting of the suffrage songs in that they set forth the arguments used by the suffragists and refute the arguments of the anti-suffragists. These songs actively integrate the rhetoric and musical styles of the period in an attempt to convince the listeners of the righteousness of the cause and to move them to action.

At the time *Let Us All Speak our Minds If We Die for it* was written it was improper for women to speak in public. This photo was taken on National Suffrage Day May 2, 1918 when the Suffrage Movement finally became popular and women were speaking their minds.

LET US ALL SPEAK OUR MINDS IF WE DIE FOR IT - William Brough / J. Gaspard Maeder

This song, written in 1863, is one of the earliest feminist songs and it is also one of the most militant. The song does not actually mention voting or suffrage, yet it is categorized as a suffrage song since suffrage was one of the main causes propounded by early women's rightists. In the program notes to "Songs of the Suffragettes" this song is described as "...the most outspoken feminist musical statement which we have been able to find." And in "Songs of Yesterday" Jordan and Kessler state that,

> *The songs of women's independence were both applauded and hissed during America's coming of age, but none received more defiant approval or contempt than the song of the militant feminist, "Let Us All Speak Our Minds if We Die for It."* (Jordan and Kessler, p. 162)

"Let Us All Speak Our Minds . . ." is a powerful feminist statement that could just as easily be sung today to the accompaniment of a guitar by a woman wearing jeans, as it was sung to the accompaniment of the piano in the 19th century by genteel ladies wearing hoop-skirts.

An irony of this song is that it fits within the genre of "Parlor Songs," which were overly sentimental and romantic, oftentimes glorifying femininity and domestic life for women. These songs usually had a moral to them since Victorians believed that women were morally superior and more innocent than men. The "MORAL" stated on the songsheet of *this* song, however, is blatantly defiant and militant, particularly considering that at the time this song was written, it was improper for women to speak in public.

Secularized music was just making its way into middle class and upper class parlors in America at the time this song was written. In her thesis, *The Image of Women in Nineteenth Century Parlor Songs*, Lori Deter describes the role this music had for women during that era:

> *Sentimental ballads, also labeled as parlor songs, became . . . a symbol of the rising middle class and the medium through which the Victorian escapist world was most vividly depicted. Ownership of a piano, in fact, was instrumental in defining a Victorian families'[sic] status, and indeed, by the middle of the century had become more the norm than the exception among middle class families. In 1829 there were 2,500 pianos manufactured in the United States. Thirty years later than number had increased by almost ten fold to 21,000.* (Deter, p. 5)

Another aspect of Let Us All Speak Our Minds . . . " which indicates that it fits within the parlor song genre is that it was written for a specific singer, *Mrs. John Wood,* as reflected on the song sheet cover. This was a common practice of parlor songs according to Deter:

> *Originally parlor songs were written for reputable singers, who introduced the most recent ballads in music halls, rather than in the family drawing room. The public, in turn, purchased the sheet music for home enjoyment. Just as it was the performers who popularized the songs, it was they, too, who received most of the benefits. More often than not during the Victorian era, it was the performer who profited from royalties and increased fame for introducing the latest "hit."* (Deter, p. 8-9)

Let Us All Speak Our Minds If We Die For It

Words: W.M. Brough

Music: J.G. Maeder

why for it— But I don't and I can't, and I won't and I shant! No, I will speak my mind if I die for it!

For we know it's all fudge, to say

man's the best judge Of what should be, and should 'nt and so on, That wo-man should bow, nor at - tempt to say how She con-

sid-ers that mat-ters should go on; I ne-ver yet gave up my-self thus a slave, How-ev- er my hus-band might

try for it For I can't and I won't, and I shant and I don't, But I will speak my mind if I die for it!

MORAL

And all la-dies I hope who've with hus-bands to cope, With the rights of the sex will not tri-fle, We all, if we choose our tongues but to use, Can all op-po-si-tion soon sti-fle; Let man if he will then bid us be still And si-lent, a price he'll pay

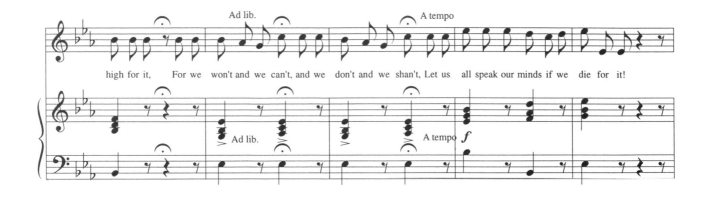

high for it,   For we won't and we can't, and we don't and we shan't, Let us   all speak our minds if we die for it!

The militant flamboyant attitude reflected in *Let Us All Speak Our Minds If We Die for It* was actualized nearly forty-five years later by Alice Paul and the National Woman's Party (NWP). Protest demonstrations included women who picketed the front gates of the White House bearing inflamatory banners, some signs declaring the President as "Kaiser Wilson."

Finally, the women were arrested for the trumped up charge of "obstructing traffic." In *Women Together* Judith Papachristou describes the arrests:

During the Summer and Fall, as picketing and rioting continued, more arrests were made. Eventually 218 women were arrested and 97 of them were sent to jail . . . The arrests of large numbers of respectable women and their incarceration in the workhouse were themselves startling events. But subsequent stories of physical abuse, the force feeding of Alice Paul and others, and the much-publicized "Night of Terror" tinged the suffragists with martyrdom (Papachristou, 179-180).

Suffragist prisoner on straw pallets on jail floor. (NWP)

In *One Woman One Vote* . . . Marjorie Spruill Wheeler depicts the "Night of Terror" in detail:

. . . thirty-three NWP women, arrested for picketing the White House . . . suffered Superintendent Whittaker's infamous "night of terror." The terror began when two soldiers attacked the picketing Boston matron Agnes Morey, jabbing her broken, splintered banner pole between her eyes. Philadelphia grandmother Dora Lewis, always in the forefront, was knocked about by three youths . . . . After the women were taken to Occoquan Workhouse . . . the guards seemed in a frenzy of rage . . . . When the other women suspected Cosu had had a heart attack, their cries to Whittaker's guards for help were ignored. NWP vice president Lucy Burns. . . . was singled out for especially rough treatment. When she resisted being hauled away, she was beaten and then eventually had her wrists hand-cuffed high on her cell door . . . she naturally tried to pull away from the guards, so they responded by pinching her arms, twisting her wrists, then wrestling her down over an iron bench, bruising her back and shoulders. One man had his hand at her throat . . . they were not even allowed to use a toilet . . . . the hunger strike was met by the counterforce of "forcible feeding" . . . . Feeding was done with tubing forced down the mouth or nostrils. Rose Winslow, who experienced forcible feeding three times a day during her imprisonment, smuggled out notes saying:

I had a nervous time of it, gasping a long time afterward, and my stomach rejecting during the process....The poor soul who fed me got liberally besprinkled during the process. I heard myself making the most hideous sounds....One feels so forsaken when one lies prone and people shove a pipe down one's stomach....I was vomiting continually during the process.The tube had developed an irritation somewhere that is painful .... It is horrible. (Wheeler, 286-287)

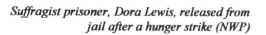

Suffragist prisoner, Dora Lewis, released from jail after a hunger strike (NWP)

The demure Victorian ladies who sang "Let Us All Speak Our Minds If We Die for It" had no inkling of the maltreatment that would occur half a decade later by women speaking their minds about suffrage. These women did not "die for it," but they surely suffered.

GOING TO THE POLLS - Julia B. Nelson to the tune of "Comin' Thro' the Rye"

Irish and Scottish songs became increasingly popular at the turn of the century, so many of these melodies were well-known to suffragists and have endured even to this day. Robert Burns fitted his own poems to folk tunes which were first published in *Scots Musical Museum* in 1787. The American Publication of *Comin' Thro' the Rye* by Burns is dated 1828. The tune is from a genuine strathspey, which is a Scottish dance in quadruple meter. The music as published here has the typical "scotch snap" rhythm which the vocalist may want to eliminate when singing *Going to the Polls*.

The lyrics of *Going to the Polls*, like many other suffrage songs, assert that once women go to the polls they will use the ballot for social and moral reform. This song goes one step further by claiming a woman has her "Bible-marching orders" to go to the polls. The song also refutes the notion expounded by the antis that the polls were places which would sully and corrupt women.

In this song, circa 1884, it is specifically mentioned that women going to the polls will "put down the liquor traffic." There was a link between suffrage and temperance in that many suffragists were also in favor of liquor reform. Some temperance songs even doubled as suffrage songs, such as the popular sentimental ballad, *Where Are Your Boys Today* .(In this song the "boys" are down at the bar while their children are starving.The final chrorus proclaims that "We will save your boys today.") However there were those who were not in favor of the temperance campaign and felt that the connection of suffrage to prohibition was harmful to the cause of suffrage. This issue served to divide suffragists.

Yet the liquor interests were clear on how they stood on the subject of suffrage. The large breweries spent a lot of money and effort campaigning against suffrage by appealing to men who liked to swill.

Going To The Polls

Words: Julia B. Nelson

Music: Comin' Thro' the Rye

If the men should see the women Going to the polls, To put down the liquor traffic Need it vex their souls? If we're an-gels, as they tell us can we once sup—pose That all the men would frown on us When go-ing to the polls. We

love our boys! our house- hold joys! We Love our girls as well. The

law of love is from a- bove, 'Gainst that we ne'er re- bel.

No discharge have Christian women
From the war with sin;
At the polls with Gog and Magog
Must the fight begin.
Since we've Bible-marching orders,
Need it fright our souls,
Though all the men should frown on us
When going to the polls?

CHORUS
We love our boys, our household joys!
We love our girls as well;
The law of love is from above,
'Gainst that we ne'er rebel.

Is This Picture So Shocking?

KEEP WOMAN IN HER SPHERE - D. Estabrook to the tune of "Auld Lang Syne"

Auld Lang Syne is one of the songs which first appeared in the first volume of Robert Burns' *Scots Musical Museum* . Like *Comin' Thro' the Rye, Auld Lang Syne* is also considered an ancient strathspey with words partly traditional and partly by Burns. Before becoming the theme song of the New Year and other occasions, it was one of the songs which Civil War soldiers carried around with them in their songsters. In *A History of Popular Music,* Sigmund Spaeth asserts that "It is still one of the world's most popular melodies, with an effective trick of seeming to unwind a five-tone pattern and then wind it up again." (Spaeth, p. 54)

At the Polls: Your Place is at Home

Keep Woman In Her Sphere was one of the most popular of the suffrage songs, being widely sung at suffrage rallies and other events. The structural pattern of the lyrics fits rather neatly into the "situation remedy structure" of the "magnetic song of persuasion" as described by Denisoff in *Sing a Song of Social Significance:*

> *This strucure is a classic form of stating and describing a situation in negative terms, like the exploitive boss, the warmonger, and the brutal law-enforcment official. Stating a situation in negative terms, the performer customarily states the solution to the social condition in the final verses."* (Denisoff, p. 7)

In *Keep Woman in Her Sphere*, the "negative terms" are the bigoted neighbor of the first verse and the drunk of the second verse. Even modern day audiences can laugh at the sarcasm of the souse who staggers from the bar and proclaims that "I've taught my wife to know her place." The "solution," to *Let woman choose her sphere,* is spoken by the "thoughtful" man in the last verse.

Keep Woman in her Sphere

Words: D. Estabrook

Music: Auld Lang Syne

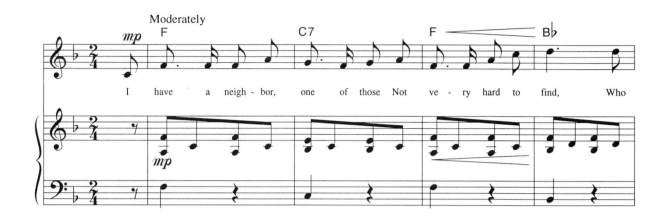

I have a neigh-bor, one of those Not ve-ry hard to find, Who

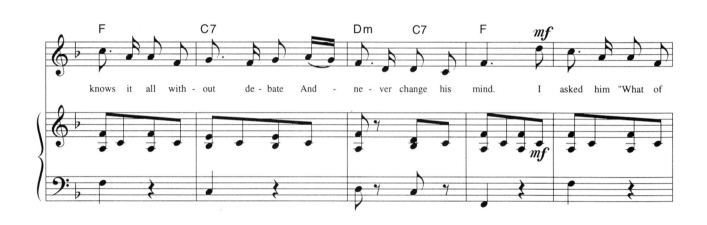

knows it all with-out de-bate And ne-ver change his mind. I asked him "What of

wo-men's rights?" He said in tones se-vere "My mind on that is all made up, Keep - wo-man in her sphere."

I saw a man in tattered garb
Forth from the grog-shop come;
He squandered all his cash for drink,
And starved his wife at home;
I asked him "Should not woman vote?"
He answered with a sneer --
I've taught my wife to know her place,
Keep woman in her sphere."

I met an earnest, thoughtful man,
Not many days ago,
Who pondered deep all human law
The honest truth to know;
I asked him "What of woman's cause?"
The answer came sincere --
"Her rights are just the same as mine,
Let woman choose her sphere."

She wont be happy till she gets it!

"The Sphere of Woman" was a "hot" issue in the Nineteenth Century and was much more than the mere modern day adage of "Woman's place is in the home." Lectures were delivered, books were written, sermons were preached, and debates were presented on the subject.

To the more robust constitution of man are appointed the labors and dangers of the chase, the toils of the field, the perils of the ocean. There is to correspond to that robuster form, a corresponding energy, enterprise, and courage. To woman the care of the home, the preparation of food, the making of clothing, the nursing and education of children. To her is given in larger measure sensibility, tenderness, patience . . . . These instincts are the unerring guide of what both man and woman ought to be. (To the left, Burnap, p. 46)

She feels herself weak and timid . . . . She needs a protector . . . . She is in a measure dependent. She asks for wisdom, constancy, firmness, perseverance, and she is willing to repay it all by the surrender of the full treasure of her affections. Woman despises in man every thing like herself except a tender heart. It is enough that she is effeminate and weak; she does not want another like herself. (Above, Burnap p. 46)

THE TAXATION TYRANNY - General E. Estabrook to the tune of "Red White and Blue"

The melody of "Red White and Blue" has withstood the test of time as a popular American tune. In *History of Popular Music* David Ewen summarizes the controversial history of the song, which is also known as "Columbia, the Gem of the Ocean."

> *Whether the melody of "Columbia, the Gem of the Ocean" is of English or American origin is a question long hotly debated but never satisfactorily resolved. Some claim that the tune came from "Britannia, the Pride of the Ocean," written by Stephen J. Meany and Thomas E. Williams in 1842. After "Columbia, the Gem of the Ocean" had been successfully introduced at the Chinese Museum in Philadelphia in 1843 by the actor-singer, David T. Shaw, Thomas A. Beckett insisted he was author of both its lyrics and music, having been commissioned by Shaw to write them. Beckett's claim notwithstanding, "Columbia the Gem of the Ocean" was first published in Philadelphia in 1843, crediting David T. Shaw as its sole author. Beckett hotly disputed Shaw's right to be considered the song's creator, and when a second Philadelphia publisher issued the song, the title page bore the legend that this was "A Popular Song . . . Adapted & Arranged by T.A. Beckett." If this publication was issued with Beckett's consent, the conclusion is justifiable that Beckett was now ready to concede that, though the lyrics were his, the melody had been borrowed. This already confused situation is even further complicated by the fact that when "Columbia, the Gem of the Ocean" was first issued in New York in 1861 -- under a changed title, "The Red White and Blue" -- it was described as a "National Song . . . Arranged by Thos. D. Sullivan." No mention was made of either Shaw or Beckett.* (Ewen, p. 14)

Regardless of who wrote "Red White and Blue," the adaptation of the melody to "Taxation Tyranny" serves to evoke the emotions of patriotism.

The lyrics also profess patriotism by referring to the Revolutionary War and the injustice of "taxation without representation" echoed by American women who were taxed, yet not allowed to vote. In referring to this song in *Sing Out*, Irwin Silber alludes to the original participants of the Boston Tea Party:

A MODERN WOMAN'S TASK.

When the Patriots of Boston in 1773 chanted "Taxation Without Representation is tyranny," they didn't dream that the argument would ever be used by their female descendants in demanding the right to vote. But that's just what they did, to the tune of "Red White and Blue" in a song called "The Taxation Tyranny." (*Sing Out*, Silber p. 8)

The Taxation Tyranny

Words: General E. Estabrook

Music: Red, White and Blue

To tax one who's not rep - re - sent - ed Is ty - ran - ny toll, if you can, Why wom - an should not have the bal - lot, She's taxed just the same as a man. King George, you re - mem - ber, de - nied us. The bal - lot, but sent us the

That one man shall not rule another,
Unless by that other's consent,
Is the principle deep underlying
The framework of this government.
So, as woman is punished for breaking
The laws which she cannot gainsay,
Let us give her a voice in the making,
Or ask her no more to obey.

CHORUS
Then to justice let's ever be true,
To each citizen render his due.
Equal rights and protection forever
To all 'neath the Red, White and Blue!

The Suffragist

FIVE CENTS

JANUARY 30, 1915

WEEKLY ORGAN OF THE
CONGRESSIONAL UNION FOR WOMAN SUFFRAGE

"THE SPIRIT OF '76"
On to the Senate!

UNCLE SAM'S WEDDING - May Wheeler to the tune of "Yankee Doodle"

The first American popular tune is said to be "Yankee Doodle." Nobody knows exactly where it came from, or specifically how old it is, but some believe that it originated in England as an instrumental piece, while others trace it back to Scotland, Ireland, Holland, or Germany. The song's introduction to the American colonies, however, is related by David Ewen:

> There is reason to believe that the melody of "Yankee Doodle" made its appearance in the colonies for the first time during the French and Indian War. In or about 1755, Richard Shuckburg, a British army physician, was so amused at the ragged and disheveled appearance of General Braddock's colonial soldiers that he decied to perpetuate a joke on them. He improvised a set of nonsense lyrics to a tune he had heard in England and palmed it off on the colonial soldiers as the latest English army song. Dr. Shuckburg's nonsense song, "Yankee Doodle," made a strong impression on the British troops in the colonies. During the next two dedcades the British often used it to taunt the colonists, sometimes by singing it loudly outside church during colonial religious services. (Ewen, p. 5)

> The Yankees soon turned the tables. When the British troops marched out of Boston on an April night in 1775, bound for Lexington to capture John Hancock and Samuel Adams, they kept step to the strains of "Yankee Doodle." At Concord the British were routed with "Yankee Doodle," as well as Yankee fire, and forever after it was to be an American song. (Howard and Bellows, p. 60)

So "Yankee Doodle" could also be said to be the first American protest song. Ewen points out the importance of music in fostering revolution:

> The significance of "Yankee Doodle" as a war song of the colonists points up the role played by popular music during the Revolution. Joel Barlow wrote in 1775: "One good song is worth a dozen addresses or proclamations." (Ewen, p. 6)

And the tune has been used to further just about every cause imaginable. It has become the most frequently adapted American melody. At least four different sets of suffrage lyrics were written to the melody of "Yankee Doodle;" "Uncle Sam's Wedding" was by far the most popular.

The lyrics to "Uncle Sam's Wedding" declare the concept that once women get the vote, they will clean up the government just as they clean their own homes.This notion was one way that suffragists could " keep woman in her sphere" and have her vote at the same time. What better status than to be the wife of Uncle Sam!

Uncle Sam's Wedding

Words: May Wheeler

Music: Yankee Doodle
Arranged by Bjorn Mercer

Of all the songs that have been sung With - in the States and nat - ion, There's none that comes so
When Un - cle Sam set up his house, He wel-comed ev - ry bro - ther, But in the haste of

near the heart As Un-cle Sam's re - la - tion. Yan - kee Doo - dle is his name, U. - S. his honored
his new life He quite for - got his mo - ther. Now his house is up in arms, A kee - per he

sta - tion. Red and white and star - ry blue His garb on each oc - ca - sion.
must find him. To sweep and dust and set to rights The tan - gles all a - bout him.

Uncle Sam is long in years
And he is growing wiser;
He now can see 'twas a mistake
To have no Miss-advisor.
His nephews now have got the reins,
And looking o'er their shoulder --
Shout to lonely Uncle Sam,
Goodbye, old man, forever."

Now we're here dear Uncle Sam
To help you in your trouble;
And the first thing best to do
Is making you a double.
Yankee Doodle will be glad,
To join with us in spreading
The news abroad o'er all the land
Of Uncle Sam's great wedding.

Following Jane Addams, Aileen Kraditor highlights the issue of "housekeeping on a large scale," where:

The modern city performs functions that necessitate the women's vote; a woman cannot care properly for her family if she has no voice in making the laws and electing the officials that determine whether her home has pure water, fresh food, proper sanitation, and adequate police protection; municipal government is housekeeping on a large scale (Kraditor, p. 116).

VOL. VI, No. 3
FIVE CENTS

The Suffragist

OFFICIAL WEEKLY ORGAN OF
THE NATIONAL WOMAN'S PARTY

SATURDAY, JANUARY 19, 1918

VICTORY NUMBER

Kirby, in the New York World, January 11

Here Comes the Bride!

OH, DEAR, WHAT CAN THE MATTER BE? - L. May Wheeler to the tune of "Oh, Dear, What Can the Matter Be?"

The original song, "Oh, Dear, What Can the Matter Be?" appeared in *The Federal Overture* in 1794 along with the first American printing of "Yankee Doodle." The strain became a popular imported tune among the American colonists. This light romantic song dates back to the reign of Henry VIII, 1509-47.

===================

The suffragist adaptation of "Oh, Dear, What Can the Matter Be?" provides a litany of what women do in society and the roles they perform. It then repeats the rhetorical question in each refrain, "Why are they wanting to vote?." The lyrics create the suppositions which the anti's often made that, since women are "protected" by husbands and "directed" by sons, they can pray, and dress for society, and work in their homes, and gossip with the neighbor, and travel, and even work outside the home, so "Why are they wanting to vote?"

The final verse changes to the more personal first person and attempts to answer the questions posed in the previous verses by concluding that "Women have labored *your* country to save," and "That's why we're wanting to vote!"

===================

In referring to the "specific song of persuasion" Denisoff comments that "most of these songs do not transcend the historical context of the lyric" (p. 7), and this certainly seems to be the case with "Oh, Dear, What Can the Matter Be?." These outdated lyrics may seem silly and no longer relevant to the modern woman, but they were pertinent at the time the song was written, circa 1884.

Part of the focus of this song though lies in the fact that it actually *does* point out how silly it was that women couldn't vote when they already did so many other things which contributed to society. It is inconceivable for us today to suppose that just a century ago people seriously suggested that women should not vote simply because they already possessed the privileges belonging to the female class.

Oh Dear, What Can the Matter Be?

Words: L. May Wheeler

Music: Oh Dear, What Can the Matter Be?

Oh, dear! What can the mat-ter be? Dear, Dear, what can the mat-ter be?

Oh, dear! What can the mat-ter be? Wom-en are want-ing the vote,_____

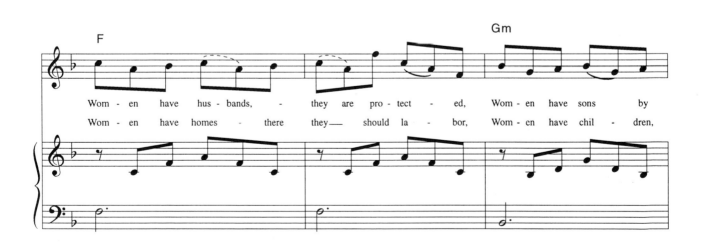

Wom-en have hus-bands, - they are pro-tect - ed, Wom-en have sons by

Wom-en have homes - there they__ should la - bor, Wom-en have chil - dren,

whom they're di - rect - ed, Wom - en have fa - thers they're not ne - glect - ed,
whom they should fav - or, Wom - en have times to— learn of each neigh - bor,

Why are they want - ing the vote?_____
Why are they want - ing to vote?_____

AW. LET 'EM SING AN' PRAY —WE GOT TH' VOTES AN' MAKE TH' LAWS

Women can dress, they love society,
Women have cash, with its variety,
Women can pray, with sweetest piety,
Why are they wanting to vote?

Women are preaching to sinners today,
Women are healing the sick by the way,
Women are dealing out law as they may,
Why are they wanting to vote?

Women are trav'ling about, here and there,
Women are working like men everywhere,
Women are crowding -- then claiming 'tis fair --
Why are they wanting to vote?

Women have reared all the sons of the brave,
Women have labored *your* country to save,
That's why we're wanting to vote!

CHORUS
Oh dear, what can the matter be:
Dear, dear, what can the matter be?
Oh dear, what can the matter be?
When men want every vote.

WINNING THE VOTE - (A.K.A. "Woman's Rights) A. B. Smith, 1912 and M. B. Slade, 1897 to the tune of "Not for Joseph"

The original tune, "Not for Joseph" was a comic song by Arthur Lloyd, a composer of the English school. The tune was "one of several songs . . . used in a modern revival of Mrs. Anna Cora Mowatt's absurd play, *Fashion*, which first appeared in 1855, but returned to the boards from time to time" (Spaeth, 170). The strain makes use of the musical dialogue which was typical of the style of songs of pre World War I America.

In the program notes of *Songs of the Suffragettes* it is stated that the 1912 edition of *Winning the Vote* suggests that "the song is more effective if acted." The notes credit the song to, " Mrs. Smith in 1912 . . . published that same year by the Busy World Publishing Co., of Madison, Wisconsin." A later rendition published in 1971 in *The Liberated Woman's Songbook* also attributes the lyrics to Mrs. Smith, 1912. However an even earlier 1897 version of the song appears in *A Woman Suffrage Leaflet* under the title, "Woman's Rights" with the lyricist listed as, M .B. C. Slade. What is presented here is an amalgamation of all three versions.

The lyrics of the three renditions vary slightly. For example, the 1897 version begins with, "I've been down to *Boston* . . .," whereas the 1912 rendition published in Madison, Wisconsin begins with "I've been down to *Madison . . . .*" Other single words are changed such as, "just as my old *coat* . . ." in the 1897 version (which logically rhymes with *vote*) becomes "just as my old *hat*" in the later versions.

The meaning is altered within the second verse of the song. In the 1897 version the lyrics warn Joseph that if he doesn't support woman's rights, the girls will not vote for him when they do win the vote:

> *Tell us Joseph, why not we should vote as well as you?/ What is there is we girls but try, we can't make out to do? / Ah, but we shall surely win the chance and now we'll let you know, / that if you don't our cause advance we'll vote but not for Joe.*

The second 1912 version uses this same second verse to present a taxation argument:

> *Say, friend Joseph, why not we should vote as well as you? / Are there no problems in the State that need our wisdom too? / We must pay our taxes same as you; as citizens be true. / And if some wicked thing we do to jail we're sent by you.*

In the *Liberated Woman's Songbook* a final "solution" verse is tacked on (presented here) which serves to make the song fit the "situation comedy structure" referred to in *Sing A Song of Social Significance*. This is the same structure used in *Keep Woman in Her Sphere* whereby "stating a situation in negative terms, the performer . . . states the solution to the social condition in the final verses" (Denisoff, p. 7). In the final verse added here, Joseph "gives in" and agrees to help the women win the vote, and then girls and boys all sing together, *We'll together soon be voters. / Yes we will, if you'll all / Vote "Yes" at the polls next fall* [sic]"

It is unknown who wrote this last verse or when it was added, but the variances of the lyrics and the changes to the words of *Winning the Vote* show how this song, in the true folk song tradition, has been passed down and adapted throughout time.

Winning the Vote

Words: M.B.C. Slade, 1897
and Mrs. A.B. Smith, 1912

Music: "Not for Joseph"
by Arthur Loyd

(Boy)1.I've been down to Bos- ton, boys, To see the folks and
(Girl)2.Tell us Jo - seph why not we Should vote as well as

sights Dear me, I heard such fuss and noise a - bout the wo - man's rights. Now 'tis
you? Are there no pro - blems in the State that need our wis - dom too? We must

just as plain as my old coat, that's plain as plain can be, That when the wo - men
pay our tax - es same as you; as cit - i - zens be true, And if some wick - ed

CHORUS

want to vote, they'll get no help from me! (Boy) Not from Joe, not from Joe,
thing we do, to jail we're sent by you. (Girl) Yes we are, same as you;

Boys

Now young women, just look here, your home is your true place
You never ought from out your sphere to show your pretty face.
Don't you know you ought to knit and sew and meek and humble be?
If from your sphere you wander so you'll get no help from me!
Help from Joe? Help from Joe?
If he knows it, not from Joseph;
No, no, no, not from Joe;
Not from me, I tell you no!

Girls

Joseph, tell us something new; we're tired of that old song:
We'll sew the seams and cook the meals, to vote won't take us long.
We will help clean house, the one too large for man to clean alone,
The State and Nation, don't you see, when we the vote have won.
Yes we will, and you'll help
For you'll need our help, friend Joseph
Yes you will, when we're in,
So you'd better help us win.

Boys

You're just right - how blind I've been, I ne'er had seen it thus;
Tis true that taxes you must pay without a word of fuss;
You are subject to the laws men made, and yet no word or note,
Can you sing out where it will count — I'LL HELP YOU WIN THE VOTE!
Yes I will. (Girls) Thank you Joe.
(All) We'll together soon be voters.
Yes we will, if you'll all
Vote "Yes" at the polls next Fall.

FEMALE SUFFRAGE - R. A. Cohen and A. J. Phelps

This pleasant, simplistic tune, written in 1867 and published by P. L. Huyett & Son in Saint Joseph, Missouri, works today with either piano or guitar accompaniment. The melody itself is of no particular distinction, but rather serves as a vehicle to present the message of the lyrics.

The satirical lyrics point out how ridiculous the anti-suffragist arguments were, simply by sarcastically enumerating them. The words are sung as if from the point of view of an anti-suffragist asserting all of the reasons why women should not vote.

There were, in fact, anti-suffrage songs written with such titles as, *The Anti-Suffrage Rose, Put Me on An Island Where the Girls are Few,* and, *Come Home Mother.* The anti-suffrage logic satirized here in *Female Suffrage* was actually put forth in songs and literature against votes for women.

Female Suffrage

Music: A.J. Phelps

Words: R.A. Cohen

coat. In fact, my charm-ing crea——tures. Do ev-'ry thing but
wrote, And clear-ly they de-fined.—— it, That man, a-lone, should

vote.
vote. You may vis - it ball and con-cert. In gau-dy hat and

coat. In fact, my charm-ing crea- tures, Do ev-'ry thing but vote.

You wish to be our equal
We prize you something more,
And proudly look upon you
Than angels little lower.
We would not have you equal,
But superior to us;
A something we can idolize
Though fashioned out of dust.

But when from her position
A careless woman's hurled,
She's the loathing of our manhood,
The scorn of all the world;
She loses her identity,
With all that's noble, then,
And seeks the common level
Of the commonest of men.

I have given my opinion,
And I hold that it is true --
What would strengthen politicians
Would tend to weaken you.
It would bring you to its level,
In spite of all that's said
And political corruption
Would show its hydra-head.

Then mothers, wives and sisters,
I beg you keep your place;
And remain what nature made you --
The help-meets of our race.
Let no temptation lead you,
Nor any wily fox,
To descend unto the level
Of the nation's ballot-box.

IS IT RIGHT - W. G. Fortney

The original melody of this song is amateurish and poorly composed. These factors combined with the dated lyrics make this song written in 1911 interesting only as a piece which represents the rhetorical context of the era. The ideas put forth in *Is It Right?* expose the fear and prejudice of the foreign-born, which was a commonly expressed attitude of the time among both suffragists and anti-suffragists who were primarily white middle class women.

Is It Right?

The irony of this title arises from the question which is likely to come to mind today when reading the lyrics of this song: *Is it Right to play upon prejudices and fears in order to promote a cause?* This is exactly what suffragists *and* anti-suffragists did in the late 19th and early 20th century. They were expressing their own concerns over the millions of immigrants arriving in America who were infiltrating every aspect of society.

We shudder today at the blatantly prejudicial and politically incorrect lyrics of this song:
> **If it's right for the Greek and the Jap, and the Chink, / The Tramp, and poor whiskey bloat, / The pauper, the fool, and the knave, and the thief, / Why not right, for a woman to vote?**

For the anti-suffragist, the immigrant represented a threat to the ideal of the *"white, Anglo-Saxon, Protestant, sober, middle-class home in which the mother was queen of the realm . . . .*
> *The 'new immigrants' usually used Sunday for recreation; they did not eschew the use of liquor; their women sometimes worked outside the home; they rarely lived in big houses on tree-lined streets, but rather seemed to prefer overcrowded tenements in which the mother could hardly be a queen or the home a realm"* (Kraditor, p.105).

The frightened antis pleaded with their legislators not to add unfit women to the electorate by giving all women the vote.

In *The Ideas of the Woman Suffrage Movement 1890-1920* Aileen Kraditor documents how suffragists felt the same way about foreigners as did the antis:
> *The suffragists, after all, belonged more or less to the same social stratum as the antis, and . . . . They soon discovered powerful arguments 'for' woman suffrage based on the same antiforeign grounds as the antis pleas 'against' the enfranchisement of women.* (Kraditor, p. 106)

Kraditor points out how various respected suffrage leaders expressed this anti-foreign sentiment in their speeches:
> *This Government is menaced with great danger . . . . That danger lies in the votes possessed by the males in the slums of the cities, and the ignorant foreign vote . . .* Carrie Chapman Catt, 1894

> *There is no race, there is no color, there is no nationality of men who are not the sovereign rulers of American women . . .* Dr. Anna Howard Shaw, 1904 (Kraditor, p. 106-107)

However, not all suffragists adhered to this bigoted point of view. Jane Addams, for one, contended that poor immigrant women needed the franchise in order to properly feed, clothe, and protect their families. And shortly after the turn of the century when female suffrage became more widely accepted and working women became involved, suffragists adopted a new sympathetic attitude towards immigrants and were speaking on street corners in working-class neighborhoods, and union meetings, and were even distributing leaflets in foreign languages.

Is it Right?

By: W.G. Fortney

Is it
Is it
Your -
She has

right for the man who has a - cres of land, Where he rais - es the sheep and the
right for the ne - gro, the Jap, and the Chink, The tramp, and the old whis - key
own lov - ing moth - er, that nursed you for years, And - rocked your lone cra - dle at
al - ways stood by you, and al - ways been true, Your - bur - dens she helps to make

goat, Who - aids in sup - port - ing his own coun - try - men, Is it right for that man to
bloat, To be hauled in a tax - i cab down to the polls, And - there be told how they must
night, Do you think her be - low the na - tive Chi - nese, Who can vote? She can - not! Is it
light, Now she asks to be raised on a plane with the Jap, Does she ask an - y more than is

vote? Is it right, for the man who al - le - giance has sworn, Though he
vote? But the wid - ow, who gov - erns her own lit - tle farm, And
right? The wife you have pledged as your e - qual in life, And
right? If it's right for the Greek, and the Jap, and the Chink, The

has neith - er cot - nor coat, But as - sists in cre - a - ting our
pays off the mort - gage and note, Is as - sessed - to help pay the
trust her from mor - ning till night, To - gov - ern your home and your
Tramp, and - poor whis - key bloat, The - pau - per, the fool, and the

Gov - ern - ment laws, Is it right, for that man - to vote?
debts of our land, Is it right, for that wid - ow to vote?
chil - dren so dear, - But you can't trust to vote, is it right?
knave, and the thief, Why not right, for a wo - man to vote?

WHEN HELEN CASTS HER BALLOT - John Kirk and Peter J. Blast

SHE'S GOOD ENOUGH TO BE YOUR BABY'S MOTHER AND SHE'S GOOD ENOUGH
TO VOTE WITH YOU - Alfred Bryan and Herman Paley

These two songs, both written in 1916, represent the worst and the best of suffrage music. *When Helen Casts Her Ballot* was published by a local music company in San Francisco and was obviously written by amateurs, while *She's Good Enough to Be Your Baby's Mother . . .* was published by the famous firm of Jerome H. Remick, which was the company where George Gershwin apprenticed as a song-plugger. The music of *When Helen Casts Her Ballot* is stilted and staid, while the music of *She's Good Enough . . .* is lively and fits the mode of the popular music of the day (which will be discussed in the next chapter, "Popular Songs").

Both these songs qualify as *songs of persuasion* because they each present the virtues of female suffrage and depict an ideal world in which voting women bring about peace and harmony. But the lyrics to *When Helen Casts Her Ballot* prove to be every bit as bad as the music. The entire song awkwardly portrays a world of peace with such ridiculous images as "cupids gayly marching" and "General Mischief in the lead." The song goes on to profess that after Helen casts her ballot, "Fighting cruisers we will shift, /To a gallant loving courtship." On the other hand, the lyrics to *She's Good Enough To Be Your Baby's Mother . . .* are clever and satirically humorous. It is in the second, more serious verse where the hope is put forth that voting mothers will stamp out the "madness" of the man's world of "war and sadness"

This theme of an ideal, loving, and peaceful future world was frequently portrayed in rhetoric and in song by suffragists. The most noteworthy example of this kind of argument was put forth in a song entitled, *A Hundred Years Hence* written and sung by the Hutchinson family. The singing Hutchinson family of New Hampshire organized professionally in 1841 and became wildly popular, touring the country with their uniquely American repertoire. Their songs often took on the three social issues of the day: abolition, temperance, and suffrage.

The important occasion in which the Hutchinsons presented *A Hundred Years Hence* was on July 4, 1875 during the Centennial Celebration held in Philadelphia. The Declaration of Independence was to be read aloud at the ceremonies. Woman Suffrage leaders looked at this moment as their opportunity to be given a hearing, but General Hawley, who had charge of the proceedings, denied them a place on the convention platform. Susan B. Anthony and Elizabeth Cady Stanton begged that they be allowed to read their Woman's Declaration of Rights, and at the last moment invitations were reluctantly proffered to a delegation of suffragists. Susan B. Anthony and three others took advantage of the invitation and appeared at the convention, interrupted the proceedings, and passed out copies of the Declaration, while Elizabeth Cady Stanton and others held their own Centennial Convention at the Unitarian Church.

Meanwhile, the Hutchinson family arrived in force for the celebration, and

> *Immediately following the Centennial convention, they repaired to the First Unitarian Church to take an active part in the woman suffrage program . . . . The Hutchinsons were in their happiest vein, interspersing the speeches with appropriate and felicitous songs. . . . The Women's Convention was finally closed by the Hutchinsons singing 'A Hundred Years Hence'* (Brink, p. 260).

The similarly idealized world presented in *When Helen Casts Her Ballot* and *She's Good Enough to Be Your Baby's Mother* is depicted in in the lyrics of *A Hundred Years Hence*:

A Hundred Years Hence

Words: Fannie Gage   Music: John Hutchinson
Sung by the Hutchinson Family

One hundred years hence, what a change will be made,
In politics, morals, religion and trade,
In statesmen who wrangle or ride on the fence,
Those things will be altered a hundred years hence,

Our laws then will be uncompulsory rules,
Our prisons converted to national schools,
The pleasure of sinning 'tis all a pretense,
And so we will find it, a hundred years hence.

Lying, cheating and fraud will be laid on the shelf,
Men will neither get drunk, nor be bound up in self,
But all live together, good neighbors and friends,
Just as Christian folks ought to, a hundred years hence.

Oppression and war will be heard of no more
Nor the blood of a slave leave his print on our shore,
Conventions will then be a useless expense,
For we'll all go free suffrage, a hundred years hence.

Instead of speech-making to satisfy wrong,
All will join the glad chorus to sing Freedom's song;
And if the Millennium is not a pretense,
We'll all be good brothers, -- a hundred years hence.

It has been well over a hundred years since this song was written, and most of the Hutchinson's predictions have not come true. Yet in his book, *Yesterdays: Popular Song in America,* Charles Hamm extolls the role that the Hutchinson singing family played in influencing the politics and morals of the country.

It may well be that the Hutchinsons altered the course of American history, that their music hastened the confrontations and conflicts that led inexorably to the Civil War, that their songs fanned passions and created the sense of togetherness and resolve necessary to convert ideas and ideals into action (Hamm, p. 156).

The idealized worlds represented here in suffrage songs may seem unrealistic and naive by modern day standards, yet one should never underestimate the power of song to effect change.

When Helen Casts Her Ballot.

Words: John Kirk

Music: Peter J. Bast

When sis - ter Hel - en casts her bal - lot Style in war will
When sis - ter Hel - en casts her bal - lot from Fight - ing cruis - ers
When sis - ter Hel en casts her bal - lot Good - night war and

quick - ly wane, And in - stead of great big can - nons,
we will shift, To a gal - lant, lov - ing court - ship,
wel - come peace, Bid fare - well to your big air - ships,

With Cu-pid's ar - rows we'll be slain, When Hel - en casts her bal - lot.—
Down life's riv - er we shall drift, When Hel - en casts her bal - lot.— There will be
Grace - ful stork our homes will seize, When Hel - en casts her bal - lot.—

troops of cu - pids gay - ly march - ing Gen - er - al Mis - chief in the lead,

May - sie's eyes bright ar - rows flash - ing, Grace - ful Mar - garet

we must heed When Hel - en casts her bal - lot.——

She's Good Enough To Be Your Baby's Mother
And She's Good Enough To Vote With You

Words: Alfred Bryan

Music: Herman Paley

No man is bet - ter than the wife he loves,——— Her love will guide him,
Let's hope and pray some day we'll hear her say——— "Stop all your mad ness,

CHORUS
a Tempo

What - e'er be - tide him! She's good e - nough——— to love you and a - dore you,
I bring you glad - ness!"

rit.

p – f *a Tempo*

She's good e - nough - to bear your trou - bles for you; And if your tears——— were

fall - ing to - day,——— No - bo - dy else——— would kiss them a - way———

She's good e - nough—— to warm your heart with kis - ses When you are lone - some and

slower   *a Tempo*

blue,——————— She's good e - nough—— to be your ba - by's moth- er And she's

good e - nough to vote with you!   you!————————

POPULAR SONGS

WANTED, A SUFFRAGETTE

SONG
WORDS & MUSIC BY
LOUETTE B. RICHARDSON

PUBLISHED BY
LOUETTE B RICHARDSON
GREENFIELD, MASS.

THE NEW YORK SHEET MUSIC CLEARING HOUSE
141-147 W. 45 TH. ST.   NEW YORK

OH! YOU SUFFRAGETTES

INTRODUCED BY

HELEN KNOWLES

WRITTEN BY
J. J. GALLAGHER
AND
B. A. KOELLHOFFER

MELODY BY
B. A. KOELLHOFFER

ARRANGED BY
ARTHUR H. WEBERBAUER

PUBLISHED BY
B. A. KOELLHOFFER, 397 So. 21st STREET
IRVINGTON, N. J.

The DARKTOWN SUFFRAGETTE PARADE

Music by FREDERICK V. BOWERS

Lyrics by F. X. MOONEY

POPULAR EDITION
LEO. FEIST NEW YORK
ASCHERBERG HOPWOOD & CREW, LTD. LONDON ENGLAND

THAT RAGTIME SUFFRAGETTE

ZIEGFELD FOLLIES

OF 1913

AS PRESENTED AT

THE NEW AMSTERDAM THEATRE

NEW YORK

Words By
HARRY WILLIAMS

Music By
NAT. D. AYER

HARRY WILLIAMS MUSIC CO.
154 WEST 46TH STREET
NEW YORK

6

POPULAR SONGS

The songs in this section fit Charles Hamm's definition of "popular music" as put forth in his book, *Yesterdays: Popular Songs in America*. He defines a poplar song as one which is

> *written for, and most often performed by, a single voice or a small group of singers, accompanied by either a single chord-playing instrument or some sort of band, ensemble, or small orchestra; usually first performed and popularized in some form of secular stage entertainment, and afterward consumed (performed or listened to) in the home; composed and marketed with the goal of financial gain; designed to be performed by and listened to by persons of limited musical training and ability; and produced and disseminated in physical form -- as sheet music in its early history, and in various forms of mechanical reproduction in the twentieth century* (Hamm, p. xvii).

Beginning in the 1890's with the establishment of *Tin Pan Alley* in New York, popular music became big business. Sheet music was sold by the millions, and minstrel music and vaudeville spectaculars produced "hits" into the early twentieth century. Many of the songs which were being sung by the masses were in ragtime or showtune style so that most of the suffrage songs in this section are defined as "popular" partly because they reflect these fashionable musical forms.

The early twentieth century is coincidently the same time that the suffrage movement gained wide popularity. 1913 saw the formation of the National Woman's Party, and that organization began to stage parades, picket the white house, and participate in other forms of civil disobedience. In 1914 the National Federation of Women's Clubs -- which by this time included more than two million white women and women of color throughout the United States -- formally endorsed the suffrage campaign. And in 1916 NAWSA president Carrie Chapman Catt unveiled her "winning plan" for suffrage victory. Catt's plan required the coordination of activities by a vast cadre of suffrage workers in both state and local associations. Finally, in 1916 Jeannette Rankin of Montana became the first American woman elected to represent her state in the House of Representatives.

Because suffragists had infiltrated popular culture, these songs are more *about* suffragists rather than *for* suffragists, and are more concerned with the image of suffragists than they are with promoting the suffrage cause. The Suffrage Movement had finally "caught on" enough for people to be singing about it.

In fact, some of the songs are actually derogatory towards suffragists, embodying stereotypical and prejudicial attitudes which were held towards "suffragettes." The more exposure these women had, the more society had to say about them, both positive and negative. The same kind of derisive remarks first made by editorialists about the forbearers of the Suffragist Movement in 1848 after the first Women's Rights Convention was held were now being heaped upon their descendants who were marching in parades, picketing, and protesting for the cause.

The songs in this section reflect society's attitude towards Suffragists, the popular music of the day, and the movement towards final acceptance of votes for women in this country.

I'M A SUFFRAGETTE - M. Olive Drennan and M.C. Hanford

THAT SUFFRAGETTE - Pauline Russell Browne
(*Songs Sung at the Indiana State Convention of the Woman's Franchise League-Indianapolis, May 4-5 1913. - For Public Meetings, Conventions, Entertainments or Vaudeville - Pubished by Paulinie[sic] Russell Brown*)

The very word, "Suffragette" so liberally used in these songs, has an original negative connotation. To be called a "Suffragette" in the nineteenth and early twentieth century was tantamount to being called a "women's libber" in the 1960's. The word was first used by the *London Globe* as a demeaning expression referring to the militant British Suffragists. The Womens Social and Political Union then adopted the term for their newsletter. In their premiere issue published in 1913 they explain their use of the name,

> *The name 'Suffragette' first applied to members of the W.S.P.U. by the Newspapers* [sic] *has, by use and association, been purified of any opprobrium or distasteful significance it may have borne in the past. It is now a name of highest honour, and women in ever-increasing thousands bear it with pride; and until a better is invented it stands as no other word does for the independence courage, public spirit, and we may add, humour, which are the attributes of the really womanly woman* (The Suffragette, October 18, 1913, front page).

HER SPRING HAT

Both of these songs sympathetically depict the suffragist. The first song proudly proclaims in the chorus that "No matter what the others think, *I am a Suffragette.*" In this song the suffragette is depicted as an eighteen year old country girl with black hair and "jet black eyes." Her mother does all of the work while her father does the voting. In *That Suffragette* every word that could possibly rhyme with "suffragette" is used to portray the suffragette favorably. She does not set her mind on a fine "aigrette," and is not a "coquette," she doesn't "run in debt," nor does she "require a gillete," and she is not "given to fret." In fact, the last line of the first verse proclaims,

Oh, the finest little woman that you surely ever met / is that Ninteen thirteen Suffragette.

I'm a Suffragette

Words: M. Olive Drennan

Music: M.C. Hanford

jet, She sad - ly to me said,_____ "Yes,
ing, He is the one to shirk._____
man, They have to "mind the rule"_____

pa - pa votes, But ma - ma can't, Oh no, not

yet, not yet_____ No mat - ter what the

oth - ers think, I am a suf - fra - gette._____

100

That Suffragette

By: Pauline R. Browne

1.O, the Suf - fra - gette, wheth - er blonde or bru - nette is the
2.O, you of - ten meet her up - on the street, And al -

one, O don't for - get who'll nev - er run in debt; O, her mind is - n't set on a
tho' her gown is sim - ple, she is al - ways neat; In her shoes there's room for her

fine ai - grette, And you can bet that she is not a co - quette. Not
shape - ly feet And her un - paint - ed face is ve - ry sweet. If a

Mannish - e-nough to re - quire a "Gil - lette", Not bold,— not rough and not giv-en to fret; Oh, the
crowd - ed car can't af - ford— a seat, She does-n't look sour and com - plete - ly beat; Dis - po -

fin - est lit - tle wom-an that you sure-ly ev - er met— Is the Nine-teen thir-teen Suf - fra - gette.
si - tion sweet as can-dy Suf - fra - gettes are fine and dan-dy, They are wom - en you should want to greet.

"The Type Has Changed."

I'M GOING TO BE A SUFFRAGETTE - D. R. Miller and Sandy Englke

WANTED, A SUFFRAGETTE - Louette B. Richardson

As the Suffragist Movement gained momentum, society reacted to the prospect of women voters with awe, dismay, and humor. The role reversal characterized in these two songs was a theme frequently addressed by both sides. The idea of "women wearing pants" has been an analogy used from the beginning of the women's rights movement to this day. In *I'm Going to be a Suffragette* the question is crudely asked, "Do they want to vote / Wear mens pants and coat or just run the shack?"

Women did not wear pants in the 19th and early 20th centuries, although some early attempts at dress reform were made. Amelia Bloomer was a suffragist and crusader for women's rights whose name became attached to the "bloomer" costume. Bloomers were an attire of full Turkish-style trousers gathered at the ankles and worn under a shortened dress. In her book on Amelia Bloomer, Anne C. Coon elaborates on the significance of the outfit,

> *By supporting dress reform and wearing the notorious 'Bloomer costume," she became a visual symbol of woman's struggle to free herself not only from the restraints of restrictive dress, but also from the social, legal, and religious corsets and stays that bound her.* (Coon, p. 3)

The outfit also became a symbol of radicalism and was ridiculed by most. Elizabeth Cady Stanton, and other renowned suffragists wore bloomers for a time, but abandoned the apparel when it seemed to draw attention away from the more important issues which they felt needed addressing.

Harper's Monthly, August 1851

Unfortunately the bloomer attire gave critics an opportunity to poke fun and make caricatures of suffragists.

These two songs, written over 30 years later, burlesque the suffragists in much the same way as did the eighteenth-century cartoonists. *Wanted A Suffragette* paints a picture of the stay-at-home husband who "Each day will attend the matinee" while the suffragette wife will, "work till late at night" and "bring home the money." The role reversal is lampooned in the chorus with the plea, "Give me a Suffragette . . . and comfort shall be mine; the care and worry shall all be thine, / And you need not work but all the time."

The lyrics and melody of both of these songs are so poorly written that the songs, which have attempted to make suffragists seem ridiculous, have themselves become ridiculous.

I'm Going To Be A Suffragate [sic]

Words: D.R. Miller

Music: Sandy Engelke

Say! I'm up a tree, Try en-light-en me, I'm in a di-lem-ma. For my lit-tle girl
What they just de-mand, I don't un-der-stand, It is quite a puz-zle. Do they want to vote,

Has her brain a-whirl, O'er a wo-man's right. Tell me what to do,
Wear mens pants and coat or just run the shack? I can't just sur-mise,

is it some - thing new, That has struck my Em - ma? I hard - ly knew just
tho' I looked so wise, I was all a fuz - zle. When she said, Bil - ly,

what to do when I called 'round last night._____ She took tight hold of my
ain't it great and slap'd me on the Back._____ Per - haps she tried to ex -

CHORUS

Hand,_____ And sang to beat the band._____ I'm goin'_____ to
plain,_____ By sing - ing this re - frain._____

be a Suf - fra - gette, Bill_____ - ly Hear me shout Hur -

ray, Hur - ray. Now don't you

think that I am sil - ly or will waste my

time a - way The sex that

al - ways jog - gled the cra dle have got some

rights you bet. I say Hip - Hip -

Hip - Hip - Hip - Hur - ray I'm goin' to

be a Suf - ra - gette. gette.

Wanted a Suffragette

by Louette B. Richardson

Who / When / The

ev - er May or Ju - li - ette, I'm not so ver - y hard to please,_____
to the polls she goes to vote, I'll keep the house all nice and warm, Care
lat - est on - ly will do for mine, Old styles and "has beens" just pass a - long, Of -

Take the part of a Suf - fra - gette, Sup - port me while I live at ease, Give
for the cat and feed the goat, And keep the chil - dren free from harm, Each
fers of such I must de - cline, Though it may mean ten thous - and strong, To

me the love of a Suf - fra - gette, So con - stant, kind, so sin - cere and true, My
day she'll work till late at night, Bring home the mon - ey and give to me, That
see her style on march - ing day, When with the oth - ers up - on the street, Will

REFRAIN

wel - fare nev - er must for - get, While I for her will both cook and brew.
I may keep her gay and bright, Each day will at - tend the mat - i - nee. Give
give me hap - pi - ness al - ways, For style like she has is hard to beat.

me a Suf - fra - gette,_____ a Suf - fra - gette,_____ The mon - ey_____ and

comfort shall all be mine;— the care— and wor - ry shall

all be thine,— And you need not work but all the time,—

If on - ly you'll— be mine, be mine;— Sweet

Suf——— fra-gette, dear Suf - fra - gette,——— Oh, do!——— oh, do!——— Be mine, be mine,——— Dear Suf - fra - gette, sweet Suf - gra - gette.———

OH! YOU SUFFRAGETTES - B.A. Koellhoffer and Arthur H. Weberbauer

*They're growing too strenuous by jingo / These women on mischief are bent /
With brick bats they've smashed all the windows / and raided the House of Parliament!*

American suffragists never broke a window, but they were influenced greatly by the militant
tactics of the British suffragettes starting as early as Elizabeth Cady Stanton and Susan B.
Anthony who both kept track of the English suffragist scene. Later, Alice Paul was "trained" in
England before coming to the United States to form the National Woman's Party.

> *There was a very direct relation between the arch-militant Women's Social and Political
> Union (WSPU) of England and the National Woman's Party of the United States. Women
> who were very important to the woman suffrage movement had long traveled the Atlantic to
> inspire and inform each other* (Wheeler, *One Woman, One Vote*, p. 280).

Alice Paul actually "raided the House of Parliament" as *Oh! You Suffragettes* reports, alongside
British suffragists. She and her American cohort, Lucy Burns, interrupted the speeches of
Secretary Grey and Winston Churchill, and they were consequently arrested and force-fed in
England before they even started protesting in the United States.

> *Their militant experiences in England gave Paul and Burns a credibility and notoriety of
> sorts with American suffragists upon their return to the United States in 1910. . . . although
> they never did use the Pankhurst's "violent" tactics such as destroying property . . . What
> Alice Paul learned from the British movement was a . . . desire for full equality, and a
> determination to organize women to act aggressively on their demands-- to **take** their rights*
> (Wheeler, *One Woman, One Vote*, p. 281).

The lyrics of *Oh! You Suffragettes* reflects the disdain which many in the United States felt
toward the British suffragettes, referring to them as "spinsters" in "war paint." Some of these
women, such as Emeline Pankhurst, came to America to deliver speeches. Emeline turned out to
be surprisingly ladylike and mild-mannered on the podium and she ended up dispelling the
stereotype of the bat-wielding mannish suffragette, which in turn served to convert many to the
cause.

Oh! You Suffragettes

Words: J.J. Gallagher
and B.A. Koellhoffer

Melody: B.A. Koellhoffer
Arr: Arthur H. Weberbauer

Vamp Till ready

* I've come to A - mer - i - ca - from the old moth - er soil, Where the
They tell me A - mer - i - ca - is the land free for all, And

suff - ra - gette spin - sters are mak - ing things boil. I
all that you need here is plen - ty of "gall" The

*) Rhythmic incongruency according
   to original printing.

114

met some in old Eng - land near the As - cot race course, Where I
spin - sters o'er in Lon don! They have plen - ty of that,

staked all my boo - dle on a blas - ted old horse. I
think if they came here they would sure - ly grow fat. I

walked through Hurst Park like a man that's half crazed And to
don't mind the girls show - ing plen - ty of grit, They may

add to my trou - bles I' near - ly was hazed, By
all wear our trou - sers as long as they fit, But

brick bats they've smashed all the win - dows And

raid - ed the House of Par - lia - ment! They're

wear - ing men's col - lars and shirt - fronts, Less

bash - ful are these sweet Co - quettes; They're

af - ter our votes, just as well as our

notes, And our trou - sers! Oh! you, Suf - fra -

1. gettes! They're gettes!

2.

THE DARKTOWN SUFFRAGETTE'S PARADE - F. X. Mooney and Frederick V. Bowers

This song combines the comic parody of suffragette role reversal with the demeaning stereotype of blacks which was commonly portrayed in popular American music. The lyrics are designed to depict the most ridiculous image possible -- *colored* women -- who "insist that women vote," who "drink and gamble," who are "smoking cigarettes," want to "be on the police force," and "won't wash and scrub for you."

The first distinct American tunes were minstrel songs which ". . . were cut out of the same cloth: texts were in dialect, usually portraying the black person as a comical, illiterate, almost subhuman being" (*Music in the New World*, Hamm, 183). Impersonations of the stereotypical black became a permanent part of the nineteenth-century American theater, and minstrel shows became the most popular musical genre after an 1828 performance by Thomas "Daddy" Rice whereby he used the tattered rags, movements, and words of a crippled black man in his stage performance. The resulting famous musical number and the term, "Jim Crow" became the vehicle for Rice's posturing and dancing, as well as the words which came to designate segregation in American language.

Minstrel shows continued throughout the nineteenth century and gave way to an era of variety shows, or vaudeville. Negroes were still burlesqued, however, and the "Coon Song" remained a popular style into the twentieth century, with such songs as, *Coon, Coon Coon, 1901; The Darktown Poker Club, 1914;* and *Goodbye My Chocolate Soldier Boy, 1917* (Klamkin. p. 88,96). All of these songs, like **The Darktown Suffragettes Parade, 1914** depict large white-eyed, thick-lipped Negro caricatures on the covers.

That suffragettes and African-Americans should be denigrated together in one song seems appropriate given the historical connection of the women's rights movement to the civil rights movement. Early suffragists Susan B. Anthony, Elizabeth Cady Stanton, and others were ardent abolitionists and believed in universal suffrage. In fact, "It was through abolitionism that white American women realized their own inequality and began the first organized effort to change their inferior place in American life" (Papachristou, p. 3).

However in 1869 suffragists literally became divided over the "Negro suffrage" issue. Stanton and Anthony and others formed the National Woman Suffrage Association, an organization whose aims were to enfranchise *all* women *first*. Lucy Stone and others formed the American Suffrage Association which supported the Fifteenth Amendment and the granting of suffrage to black males as a first step toward gaining suffrage for all.

After the two groups united to form the NAWSA in 1890 and the suffrage movement gained momentum, there began to be a change in attitude toward universal suffrage, and the movement even took on the hue of white racism. Aileen Kraditor attributed this change to three factors:

> *First, as the woman suffrage movement advanced in popular favor, women who shared their contemporaries' opinions on every other issue joined it, bringing to the movement with them the race-consciousness that by then had become universal in American thought. . . . Second, those abolitionists who survived into the twentieth century largely accepted the new intellectual temper of the times and concluded that the Negro question and woman suffrage were really unrelated. . . . Third, Southern white women began building a suffrage movement the principal argument of which was that the enfranchisement of women would insure the permanency of white supremacy in the South* (Kraditor, p. 138-9).

The Darktown Suffragettes' Parade

Words: F.X. Mooney

Music: Frederick V. Bowers

colored po - pu - la - tion, since Lin - da An - na John - son came to
sure - ly make you diz - zy, now they've de - ci - ded to be suf - fra -

town;_____ All the wen - ches they are rea - ching for a
gettes;_____ 'Round the town till dawn they ram - ble, they've be -

brand new kind of tea - ching, And the co - lored gen - tle - men all wear a
gun to drink and gam - ble, They 've e - ven star - ted smo - king ci - ga -

frown._____ She in - sist that wo - men vote and
rettes._____ They in - sist that wo - men should be

men should go to work, She's got them worried, they'll be no end - less
on the po - lice force, And, strange to say, the men think they_ 're

strife,_ If a gal won't wash and scrub for you and
right,_ If some pret - ty wench would run them in and

slip you lots of dough, Why, - what's the use, they say, to have a
take them to the house, Why they'd glad - ly be ar - res - ted ev - 'ry

wife?_ The wen - ches are in line dressed
night._ The wen - ches are in line dressed

up they look so fine, They all de-clare,— they loud-ly swear, they'll
up they look so fine, They all de-clare— they loud-ly swear, they'll

make the men re - sign. When the Dark-town Suf - fra - gettes are on pa -
make the men re - sign.

rade———— way up in front,———— a big bri -

gade———— of the la - dy po - li - ti - cians, right be -

123

hind the swell mu - si - cians, and the men will car - ry ban - ners to dis -

play._____ We've got your goat, we want your vote, for

we are here to stay, We'll car - ry ra - zors and shoot craps, but

we must be o - beyed, We've raised the kids and raised them well, and

now you bet we'll all raise !!! When the Dark - town Surf - fra - gettes are on pa -

strike with palm
of hand

rade.

When the rade.

THAT RAGTIME SUFFRAGETTE - Harry Williams and Nat D. Ayer

This song epitomizes the integration of popular music with the suffragist theme. The theater extravaganza was at its peak in the form of the Zeigfeld follies, ragtime music was almost a national mania, and the song publishers of Tin Pan Alley were churning out hits capitalizing on both these factors. Issues of the day such as suffrage for women were often used as subjects for "ragtime" and/or vaudevillian music.

Ragtime in its purist form is strictly instrumental. A broader definition is, ". . . *a dance-based American vernacular music, featuring a syncopated melody against an even accompaniment*" (Hasse, p. 2).

Many popular songs, such as *That Ragtime Suffragette*, were actually "token" ragtime and may have only had the word "ragtime" in the title as a selling point. Hamm points out this aspect of ragtime songs:

> *. . . all the . . . ragtime songs merely "suggest" the rhythmic spirit of ragtime . . . they are brash, spirited, slightly syncopated, breezy, almost always humorous . . . A pattern was established with the ragtime song that was to recur time again in the twentieth century: white popular music skimmed off superficial stylistic elements of a type of music originating among black musicians . . .* (Hamm, *Yesterdays*, p. 320-321).

That Ragtime Suffragette was actually one of the songs used for the 1913 Zeigfeld Follies, and as was often the case for songs which were the outcome of musical theater productions, its cover features the same design as the program for the Follies of that year. The words, *As Presented at the New Amsterdam Theater*, are particularly significant since that was the first year the Follies were performed in that arena.

> *In 1913 Erlanger booked the "Follies" into the New Amsterdam Theater, indicating that the "Follies" had "arrived." This theater was New York's theatrical jewel, referred to as the "Grandest in the World" Built in 1903 for about $2 million, it was the most beautiful Art Nouveau theater in the United States* (Zeigfeld, p. 53).

The subject of the 1913 Follies was a *loose plot* which, ". . . *concerned the frivolities of white men as seen by a group of American Indians looking down at Manhattan. Satan came into the plot because he wanted to sample some of the earth's 'follies' before returning to his own realm*" (Zeigfeld, p. 54).

That Ragtime Suffragette is light and humorous in both melody and lyrics, and while it derides suffragists it lacks the blatant denigrating aspects of some of the other popular suffragist melodies. The 1913 suffragist may have heard this song and laughed along with it.

That Ragtime Suffragette

Words: Harry Williams

Music: Nat. D. Ayer

Vamp

Voice

What's the noise—— up-on the Av - e - nue?—— What's that crowd—— a - do - ing

Bands are play - ing as she swag- gers by—— Ban - ners sway - ing while the

'round there too?____ What's the rea - son for that aw - ful crash?____
men all sigh:____ "Why don't you - go home and bake a cake?

Has a tax - i cab got in a smash?____
One like dear - old moth - er used to make?____

John - nie, John - nie, run and get your gun!____ Get your gun
"Ma - ma, ma - ma," how the ba - by sighs,____ "Pa - pa, get

or you'll be dead my son!____ It would make Na -
the bot - tle," ma - ma cries,____ For you know that

CHORUS

suf - fra - gette!
Shake'em up, shake'em up, shake'em up,
Rag - ging with bomb——

shells and rag - ging with bricks,—— Hag - ging and nag - ging in

pol - i - tics, That Rag - time Suf - fra - gette!

Break'em up, break'em up, break'em up, She's no house - hold pet!——

130

While her hus - band's wait - ing home to dine———

She is rag - ging up and down the line   Shout - ing

votes, votes,   votes, votes,   votes, for wom - en, oh, you Rag - time

Suf - fra - gette!——————   That gette!——————

UPDATE: THE YELLOW RIBBON

THE YELLOW RIBBON - Marie Le Baron to the tune of "Wearing of the Green"

No one can place the authorship of the Irish melody, *Wearing of the Green*, written in 1798, but the tune has been parodied many times. It was used during the Civil War by the North for *We Are Coming Father Abraham* and just after the end of the War for *The Wearing of the Grey* (Hamm, *Yesterdays*, p. 249).

This haunting lyrical tune serves as the perfect musical setting to set forth the message of *The Yellow Ribbon*.

'Tis just a hundred years ago our mothers and our sires/
Lit up, for all the world to see, the flame of freedom's fires

The above words opening the first verse of *The Yellow Ribbon* would indicate that these lyrics were created somewhere around 1876, one hundred years after the Revolutionary War. The remainder of the song traces the contributions of women for equal rights through the civil war and up to the time the song was written.

The yellow ribbon was worn across the chest by suffragists in parades and demonstrations and had the words *Votes for Women* written on it. The yellow ribbon became more conspicuous after it was worn in the June 1916 demonstration held in St. Louis.

The National Democratic Convention held in St. Louis in June 1916, offered a splendid opportunity which both State and city suffragists eagerly seized. Some unique schemes were evolved, among them the 'golden lane,' . . . It has been described as 'a walkless, talkless parade' and consisted of about 7,000 women arranged in a double line on both sides of the street, the front row sitting, the back row standing, all dressed in white with yellow sashes and each one carrying a yellow parasol. They held their places on the opening day of the convention, June 14, from 10 a.m. till noon, on both sides of Locust Street for a distance of ten blocks, the route the delegates had to take in going from their headquarters in the Jefferson Hotel to the Coliseum, where the convention was held (Stanton, vol. 4, p. 348-348).

4   ST. LOUIS POST-DISPATCH   MONDAY EVENING, JUNE 12, 1916.

SUFFRAGE FORCES DIVIDE ON DEMANDS UPON DEMOCRATS

How Suffragists Will Look When They Line Up in the "Golden Lane" on Locust Street Wednesday

One Faction Wants Plank in Platform, Other Action by Present Congress.

MRS. CATT CONFIDENT

Believes Majority Party Will Declare for Votes for Women.

Suffragettes of the newly organized Woman's party and the National American Woman Suffrage Association today made demands for two widely different actions on their issue upon Democratic leaders.

The national organization, headed by Mrs. Carrie Chapman Catt, insisted upon a declaration for suffrage in the Democratic platform while the Woman's party representative, through its chairman, Miss Ann Martin, declared that unless the convention Resolutions Committee demands immediate adoption of the Susan B. Anthony amendment by Congress, her organization will declare war.

"There is no use to delay," Miss Martin declared today. "The party has the votes in Congress to pass this amendment if it so desires. We will present our last move and the leaders can do as they choose. The time for declarations of good intentions and

Left to right: Mmes. B. F. Burch, Frederick Taussig, George Gellhorn and W. C. Fordyce.

The Yellow Ribbon

Words: Marie Le Baron

Music: Wearing of the Green

We boast our land of freedom, the unshackling of the slaves;
We point with proud, though bleeding hearts, to myriads of graves;
They tell the story of a war that ended Slavery's night;
And still we women struggle for our Liberty, our Right.

CHORUS

UPDATE VERSE: (F. Wolff, 1997)
We have been through wars and poverty, pollution and the bomb;
Our nation needs our women to be dutiful and calm;
We remember our foremothers, Carrie Catt and Susan B.,
As we cast our votes for tolerance, for peace, and liberty.

UPDATE CHORUS: (F. Wolff, 1997)
Oh we still wear that yellow ribbon upon our woman's breast,
We are prouder of its sunny hue than of a royal crest;
Twas God's own primal color, born of purity and light,
We wear it now for justice, equal pay, and equal rights.

Photo by J.P. Liang, *Springfield News-Leader,* Springfield. MO

Jean Killough places a yellow ribbon on her 13-year-old granddaughter, Heather Fuller, for a parade held in Springfield, Missouri, August 27, 1995 to commemorate the 75th Anniversary of the passage of the 19th Amendment.

Mrs. Killough's mother marched in Hartford, Connecticut, over 75 years ago in a parade which was organized by Katherine Hepburn's mother. The legacy lives on.

In 1918 the two major suffrage organizations, the two-million-strong National American Women's Suffrage Association (NAWSA) headed by Carrie Chapman Catt and the smaller but more militant National Woman's Party (NWP) led by Alice Paul, often found themselves at odds with one another over direction and tactics.

But on January 10th "forty years to the day from the first introduction of the Susan B. Anthony Amendment in Congress" [a tactic supported primarily by the NAWSA] and "one year exactly from the time the first picket-line went to stand before the White House" [a ploy orchestrated by the NWP] the Federal Suffrage Amendment passed the House of Representatives with just one vote to spare (Irwin, p. 347).

As women poured out of the galleries a Woman's Party member from Massachusetts struck up the doxology. The marble halls reverberated to the sound of 'Praise God from which all blessings flow" **and for a few minutes NAWSA and Woman's Party members sang in harmony** (Scott and Scott, p. 42).

Two years later, a modified *Woman's Doxology* was written to celebrate the passage of the 19th Amendment.

THE WOMAN'S DOXOLOGY

By Mira H. Pitman
1920

Praise God, from whom all blessings flow.
Praise Him all women here below.
Now can we raise our voices high
And shout hosannas to the sky.
For we have won the mighty fight --
Long did we labor for the right.
And now in solemn thanks to Thee
We sing Thy praises. We are free!
Oh guide us -- teach us wisdom great,
Help us to choose the path that's straight.
Help us to make this world a place
Safe for the children of our race.

BIBLIOGRAPHY

About American Popular Music:

Brink, Carol. Harps in the Wind: The Story of the Singing Hutchinsons. New York: Macmillan Co., 1947.

Denisoff, R. Serge. Sing a Song of Social Significance. 2nd edn. Bowling Green, OH: Bowling Green State University Press, 1983.

Deter, Lori. The Image of Women in Nineteenth Century Parlor Songs. Thesis. New Orleans, Tulane University, 1981.

Ewen, David. History of Popular Music. New York: Barnes and Noble, Inc., 1961.

Hamm, Charles. Music in the New World. New York: W. W. Norton & Co., 1983.

Hamm, Charles. Yesterdays: Popular Song in America.. New York: W.W. Norton & Co., 1979.

Howard, John Tasker and George Kent Bellows. A Short History of Music in America. New York: Thomas Y. Crowell Co., 1957.

Jordan, Philip D. And Lillian Kessler. Songs of Yesterday: A Song Anthology of American Life. Garden City, New York: Doubleday, Doran & Co., 1941.

Klamkin, Marian. Old Sheet Music. New York: Hawthorne Books, Inc. 1975.

Levy, Lester S. Give Me Yesterday: American History in Song, 1890-1920. Norman, OK: University of Oklahoma Press, 1975.

Silber, Irwin. Lift Every Voice. New York, NY: Oak Publishers, 1953.

Silber, Irwin. Songs America Voted By. Harrisburg, Pennsylvania: Stackpole Books, 1971.

Spaeth, Sigmund. A History of Popular Music in America. New York: Random House, 1948.

Wenner, Hilda E. Here's To the Women: 100 Songs for and About American Women. New York: Syracuse University Press, 1987.

Wenzel, Lynn and Carol J. Binkowski. I Hear America Singing: A Nostalgic Tour of Popular Sheet Music. New York: Crown Publishers, Inc., 1989.

Ziegfeld, Richard and Paulette Ziegfeld. The Ziegfeld Touch. New York: Harry N. Abrams, Inc., 1993.

Related to American Woman Suffrage:

Benjamin, Anne Myra Goodman. A History of the Anti-Suffrage Movement in the United States from 1895-1920: Women Against Equality. Lewiston: Edwin Mellen Press, 1991.

Beeton, Beverly. Women Vote in the West: The Woman Suffrage Movement, 1969-1896. New York: Garland, Publishers, 1986.

Camhi, Jane Jerome. Women Against Women: American Anti-Suffragism, 1880-1920. Brooklyn, NY: Carlson Publishers, 1994.

Catt, Carrie Chapman. Woman Suffrage and Politics: The Inner Story of the Suffrage Movement By Carrie Chapman Catt and Nettie Rogers Shuler. Seattle, WA: University of Washington Press, 1969.

Coolidge, Olivia. Women's Rights: The Suffrage Movement in America, 1848-1920. New York: E.P. Dutton, 1966.

Coon, Anne C., ed. Hear Me Patiently: The Reform Speeches of Amelia Jenks Bloomer. Westport, CT: Greenwood Press, 1994.

Clarke, Mary Stetson. Bloomers and Ballots: Elizabeth Cady Stanton and Women's Rights. New York: Viking Press, 1972.

Greene, Dana. Suffrage and Religious Principle: Speeches and Writings of Olympia Brown. New Jersey and London: Scarecrow Press, 1983.

Ford, Linda. Iron Jawed Angels: The Suffrage Militancy of the National Woman's Party, 1912-1920. Lanham, MD: University Press of America, 1991.

Frost, Elizabeth and Kathryn Cullen-DuPont. Women's Suffrage in America: An Eyewitness Account. New York: Facts on File, 1992.

Gluck, Sherna. From Parlor to Prison: Five American Suffragists Talk About Their Lives. New York: Random House, 1976.

Graham, Sara Hunter. Woman Suffrage and the New Democracy. New Haven, CT: Yale University Press, 1976.

Gurko, M. The Ladies of Seneca Falls: The Birth of the Woman's Rights Movement. New York: Schocken Books, 1976.

Hagen, Martha Ann. The Rhetoric of the American Anti-Suffrage Movement 1867-1920. Thesis. Pulman, WA: Washington State University, 1993.

Hall, Florence Howe. Julia Ward Howe and the Woman Suffrage Movement. Boston: Dana Estes and Company Publishers, 1913.

Irwin, Inez Hayes. The Story of Alice Paul and the National Woman's Party. Fairfax, VA: Denlinger's Publishers, Ltd., 1977.

Jablonsky, Thomas J. The Home, Heaven and Mother Party: Female Anti-Suffragists in the United States, 1868-1920. Brooklyn, NY: 1994.

Jo, Mari and Paul Buhle, eds. The Concise History of Woman Suffrage: Selections from the Classic Work of Stanton, Anthony, Gage and Harper. Urbana: University of Illinois Press, 1978.

Kraditor, Aileen S. The Ideas of the Woman Suffrage Movement, 1890-1920. New York: Columbia University Press, 1965.

Meyers, Madeleine. Forward Into Light: The Struggle for Woman's Suffrage. (Textbook) Lowell, MA: Discovery Enterprises, 1994.

Porter, Kirk Harold. A History of Suffrage in the United States. 1918. Chicago: University of Chicago Press. New York: J.B. Lipponcott, Co., 1975.

Scott, Anne Firor and Andrew M. Scott. One Half the People: The Fight for Woman Suffrage. New York: J.B. Lippincott, Co., 1975.

Solomon, Martha M., ed. A Voice of Their Own: The Woman Suffrage Press, 1840-1910. Tuscaloosa: University of Alabama Press, 1991.

Stanton, Elizabeth Cady. History of Woman Suffrage. 6 vols. New York: Fowler & Wells, 1881.

Stevens, Doris. Jailed for Freedom: American Women Win the Vote. Troutdale, OR: NewSage Press, 1995.

Sullivan, George. The Day the Women Got the Vote: A Photo History of the Women's Rights Movement. New York: Scholastic Press, 1994.

Tickner, Lisa. The Spectacle of Women: Imagery of the Suffrage Campaign, 1907-14. Chicago: University of Chicago Press, 1988.

Wheeler, Marjorie Spruill, ed. One Woman One Vote: Rediscovering the Woman Suffrage Movement. Troutdale, OR: New Sage Press, 1995.

Wheeler, Marjorie Spruill. Votes for Women! The Woman Suffrage Movement in Tennessee, the South and the Nation. Knoxville: University of Tennessee Press, 1995.

Song Sources and Documents:

Bittenbender, Ada M. <u>Woman Suffrage Campaign Song Book.</u> Lincoln, NB: Tribune Print Co., 1982.

Brown, Pauline Russell. <u>Woman's Suffrage songs: For Public Meetings, Conventions, Entertainments or Vaudeville - songs Sung at the Indiana State Convention of the Woman's Franchise League, Indianapolis, Indiana May 4-5 1913</u>.

Mills, Harriet May and Isabel Howland. <u>Manual for Political Equality Clubs</u>. New York: National American Woman Suffrage Association, 1869.

Smith, Eleanor. <u>Hull House Songs</u>. Chicago: Clayton F. Summy Co, 1915.

Silber, Irwin. "Singing Suffragettes Sang for Women's Votes, Equal Rights." <u>Sing Out</u> 6.4 (1957): 4-12.

<u>Songs of the Suffragettes.</u> L.P. Folkways, 1958.

Wheeler, L. May. <u>Booklet of Song: Suffrage and Temperance Melodies</u>. Minneapolis: Minneapolis Cooperative Printing Co., 1884.

POSTSCRIPT

On June 14, 1919, the Congress of the United States finally approved the woman suffrage amendment. However, the struggle was not over as three-fourths of the states (thirty-six) had to ratify the amendment in order for it to pass. By mid-June 1920, a year after congress had sent the amendment to the states for approval, thirty-five had ratified.

Needing only one more state for ratification, suffragists were devastated when the next state to vote, New Jersey, unexpectedly joined the states who had voted against ratification. North Carolina then called a special session and it too voted against the amendment.

A special session of the Tennessee legislature was then called giving the amendment a last chance to become ratified before the November presidential elections. Suffragists and opponents poured into Nashville in August of 1920 where the final battle over suffrage was waged.

It was a wild ten days. The liquor interests, railroad lobby and manufacturers lobby were all active. Opponents of suffrage set up shop on the 8th floor of the Hermitage Hotel and dispensed Old Bourbon and moonshine whisky with lavish insistence (Scott, p. 45).

The suffragists, meanwhile, allegedly employed tactics that were more subtle but no less persuasive. 'Automobile rides, hugs, kisses . . . were frequently witnessed . . . (Wheeler, *One Woman, One Vote*, p. 345).

Suffragists gave each Tennessee legislator a yellow rose. The rose, worn on the legislator's lapel, signified "yes" for suffrage. Anti-suffragists followed with a red rose for each legislator.

When Harry T. Burn, the youngest member of the house, was about to cast the vote which would determine whether or not the Amendment would be ratified, it is rumored that his lapel sported a red rose. However, he pulled a telegram from his pocket which had been sent to him at the last moment from his mother. The text of the telegram follows:

Hurrah! And vote for suffrage and don't keep them in doubt. I notice some of the speeches against. They were very bitter. I have been watching to see how you stood, but have noticed nothing yet. Don't forget to be a good boy and help Mrs Catt put 'Rat in Ratification.

One apocryphal version has it that Harry Burns read the telegram then switched his rose to a yellow rose before he cast the vote which finally won suffrage for American women.

144